T0401445

Alex Hughes @alexskitchenbangers

LOW-CAL KITCHEN BANGERS

100 quick and easy meals to help you lose weight

Hey there,

I'm Alex, the creator behind Alex's Kitchen Bangers, and I am so, so excited that you are here reading my first published cookbook. Some of you may know me from my social media accounts, some of you may not have a clue who I am - either way let me introduce myself.

What started out as a way to improve my own eating habits and relationship with food became a way to help others. From a young age I struggled with food, believing that you had to restrict yourself to lose weight, so that's what I did. I would have extremely sad meals, often with food I didn't enjoy - some meals I would skip just so that I could be 'skinny'. Of course it would constantly backfire because I'd end up overeating to compensate for the meals I had missed.

After my backpacking days, I knew something had to change. Surely I could still eat food I enjoyed? So I started to experiment with meals in the kitchen, finding ways to make them lighter without sacrifice. I would constantly send photos of my food to my best friend, who urged me to make a social media account to share it. I didn't see any point, until one day at work. At the time I worked for the NHS, for a children's mental health service, and I had to chaperone a young girl who had an eating disorder. Sitting in that room just reminded me of how I'd felt and the struggles I had faced. I knew there were so many others out there just like us, with so many conflicting diet trends fed to us from an early age, not knowing which way to turn. So I walked out of work, went home and set up my instagram page: Alex's Kitchen Bangers.

From there I was on a mission - to change people's views and to show that you can eat carbs and lose weight. I believe recipes should be easy, exciting and fun, without sacrificing on taste. Most importantly they should be food you can sustain eating for the long run so you don't end up in a yo-yo cycle. I've also included veggie options, and for those who are conscious of their protein, I have added in suggestions so you can boost this where needed too.

I cannot wait for you to get cooking. Please share with me on social media whatever you rustle up from this book. I love to see all of your creations as well as hearing about how I have helped you.

Thank you so much for picking up this book. It really is a dream come true.

Alex

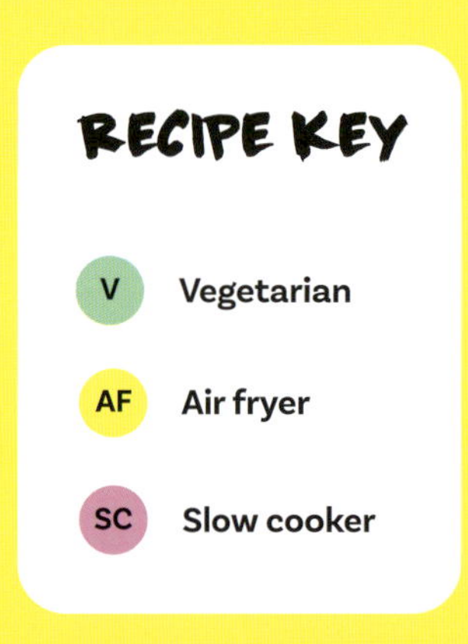

RECIPE KEY
V Vegetarian
AF Air fryer
SC Slow cooker

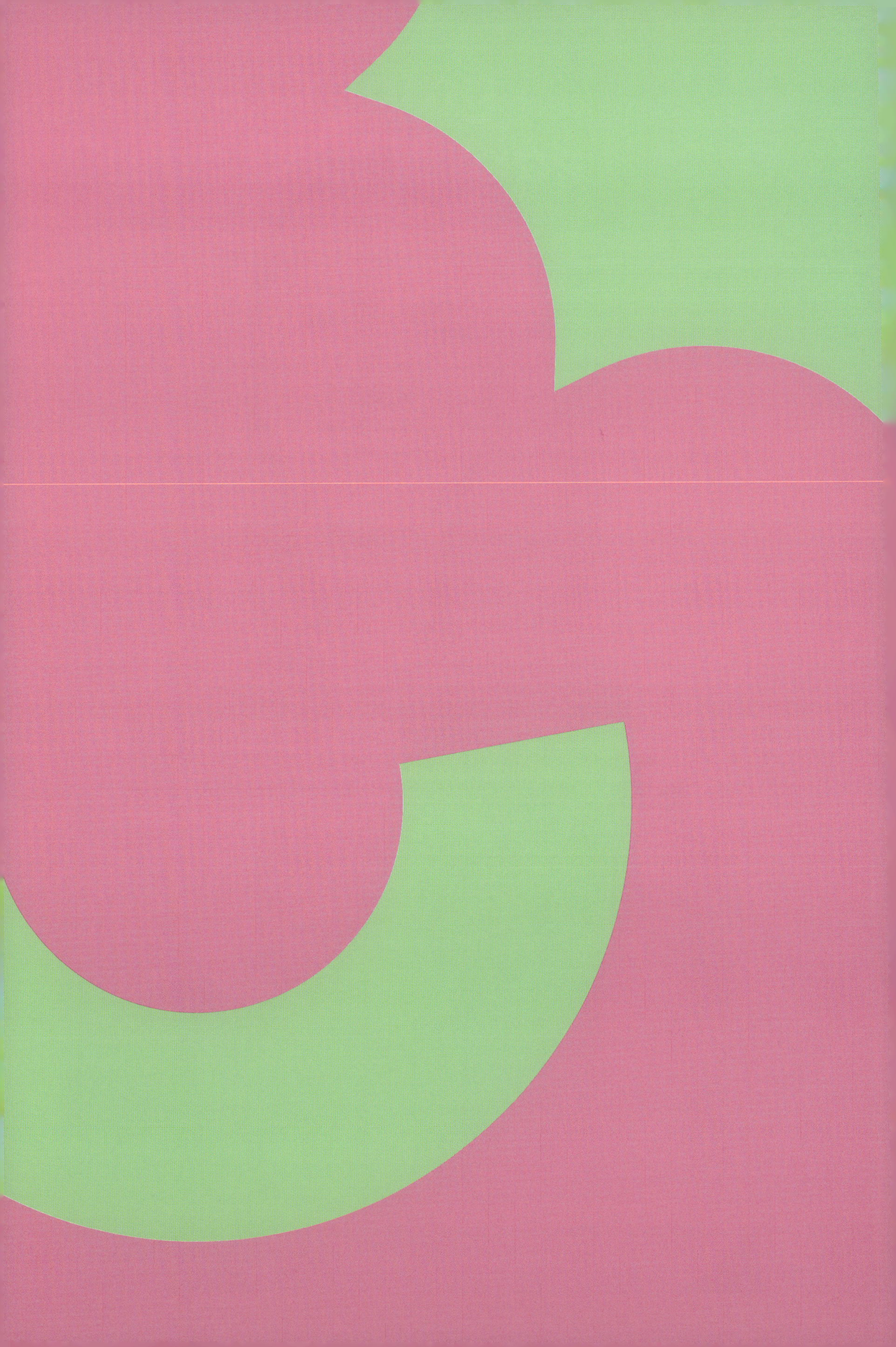

One

BANGING BREAKFASTS

Easy Prep Egg Muffins

Protein 7.5g | **Fat 5.5g** | **Carbs 1.3g**

MAKES 10
TAKES 30 minutes

There are no more excuses to skip breakfast with these egg muffins. Easily prep them at the start of the week for an on-the-go breakfast. It's a forgiving recipe, so feel free to leave out the meat or change up the veggies for whatever you have in the fridge!

Ingredients

Low calorie cooking spray (optional)

8 medium eggs

2 salad tomatoes, chopped into small pieces

Handful of spinach, chopped into small pieces

2 tbsp tomato salsa

40g chorizo, diced

40g reduced fat Cheddar, grated

½ tsp smoked paprika

1 tsp garlic granules

¼ tsp dried oregano

Salt and pepper

Method

- Preheat the oven to 180°C/160°C fan and line a 12-hole muffin tray with 10 silicone moulds. Alternatively, spray 10 muffin holes with low calorie cooking spray to ensure the muffins do not stick.
- Whisk together the eggs until combined, then add the tomatoes, spinach, salsa, chorizo and half of the Cheddar. Mix together, then season with salt and pepper, followed by the smoked paprika, garlic granules and oregano.
- Pour the batter into each muffin mould until filled. Scatter over the remaining Cheddar.
- Bake in the centre of the oven for 20 minutes. Leave the muffins to cool slightly before eating. If making ahead of time, ensure they are cooled completely before storing in the fridge for 3–4 days.

Breakfast Potatoes

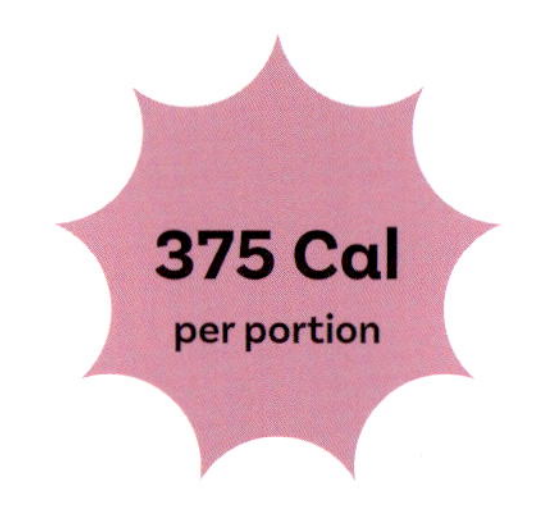

Protein 22.4g | Fat 12.9g | Carbs 43.9g

SERVES 2
TAKES 30 minutes

A pan full of fluffy potatoes finished with fried eggs and gooey melted cheese, this is the perfect brunch recipe. You could easily change the egg for scrambled if you fancy meal-prepping this recipe ahead of time for weekday breakfasts.

Ingredients

400g golden potatoes, cubed
Low calorie cooking spray
2 rashers of smoked bacon, sliced
1 small green pepper, diced
1 white onion, diced
1 tsp smoked paprika
1 tsp garlic powder
1 tsp onion powder
2 medium eggs
40g reduced fat Cheddar, grated
2 spring onions, finely chopped
A few sprigs of fresh parsley, finely chopped
Sea salt and pepper

Method

- Boil the potatoes for 15 minutes in a large pan of salted water. Drain and leave to steam dry for 5 minutes.
- Spray a large frying pan with low calorie cooking spray, add the bacon and fry over a medium heat for 5 minutes until cooked on both sides. Remove the bacon from the pan and add the green pepper and onion and cook over a medium heat for 3-4 minutes.
- Meanwhile, season the potatoes with the smoked paprika, garlic powder, onion powder, salt and pepper. Once the onion and peppers have started to soften, add the potatoes and fry for 5 minutes.
- Move the potatoes to the sides of the pan to make space for the eggs, then crack both into the centre, topping with the cheese. Leave on the heat for the eggs to cook.
- Top with the cooked bacon, spring onions and parsley.

Gochujang Egg and Chorizo Stuffed Pittas

Protein 29.0g | Fat 15.0g | Carbs 34.0g

SERVES 2
TAKES 15 minutes

If you get bored of the same old breakfast tastes, these flavour combinations will help to bring back some spark to those mundane mornings. Gochujang paste provides a red peppery base for the chorizo to really pop off. Plus, this is a breakfast you can easily meal prep to save some time in the mornings.

Ingredients

4 medium eggs
50g fat-free Greek yoghurt
1 tsp gochujang paste
1 tsp smoked paprika
20g chorizo, diced
30g reduced fat Cheddar, grated
2 pitta breads
Drizzle of sriracha sauce
1 spring onion, diced
Salt and pepper

Method

- In a bowl, whisk the eggs with the yoghurt until well combined. Then add the gochujang paste, smoked paprika and salt and pepper to taste. Set to one side.
- In a frying pan, fry off the diced chorizo pieces over a medium heat for 3–4 minutes. Remove from the pan.
- In the same frying pan, over a medium heat, add the egg mixture. Wait for a minute until the eggs start to set, then start to fold in the edges to the middle of the pan to scramble the eggs.
- Once cooked through, remove from the heat and stir through the cheese and chorizo.
- Toast the pitta breads before stuffing with the egg mixture. Finish with sriracha and spring onion for garnish.

Creamy Chilli Jam Bagel

Protein 21.0g | **Fat 6.0g** | **Carbs 61.3g**

SERVES 1
TAKES 20 minutes

The flavour combinations in this bagel are guaranteed to bring sunshine to your mornings and you can easily prep them ahead of time. Enjoy the creamy chilli sausage with a crispy hash brown, or change things up by adding diced tomato or even some chorizo!

Ingredients

2 chicken chipolatas
1 hash brown, frozen
1 bagel
25g lightest soft cream cheese
10g chilli jam
Handful of spinach

Method

- Cook the chipolatas and hash brown according to the packet instructions.
- Meanwhile, slice the bagel in half and toast until slightly browned.
- Once the chipolatas and hash brown are cooked, chop them roughly together on a chopping board. Transfer to a bowl and mix with the cream cheese and chilli jam.
- Add the spinach to one half of the bagel and top with the chicken mix and the other bagel half.

Store the chicken mix, covered, in the fridge for up to 3 days. Ensure the filling is completely cool before covering and chilling.

Breakfast Flatbread Pizza

Protein 37.1g | Fat 14.0g | Carbs 39.1g

MAKES 1
TAKES 20 minutes

Pizza for breakfast? It would be rude not to. This super easy flatbread pizza will bring a huge smile to your face (and your tummy). Mix and match any meat you fancy on the day or leave it off for a veggie-friendly version!

Ingredients

2 bacon medallions
1 tbsp tomato purée
1 tbsp reduced sugar tomato ketchup
1 tbsp water
1 flatbread
1 salad tomato, chopped
20g reduced fat Cheddar, grated
1 large egg
¼ tsp dried oregano
Salt and pepper

Method

- Preheat the oven to 200°C/180°C fan. Preheat the grill to high.
- Grill the bacon for 5–7 minutes until almost cooked. Remove and cut into small pieces.
- Mix together the tomato purée, ketchup and water until combined. Brush over the flatbread. Transfer the flatbread to a baking tray.
- Scatter the bacon, chopped tomato and half of the cheese around the edges, leaving an empty circle in the middle for the egg.
- Crack the egg into a small bowl. Carefully add it to the centre of the flatbread.
- Scatter the remaining cheese all over the flatbread. Season with the oregano and salt and pepper.
- Bake in the oven for 8–10 minutes or until the egg white has set.

Folded Breakfast Wrap

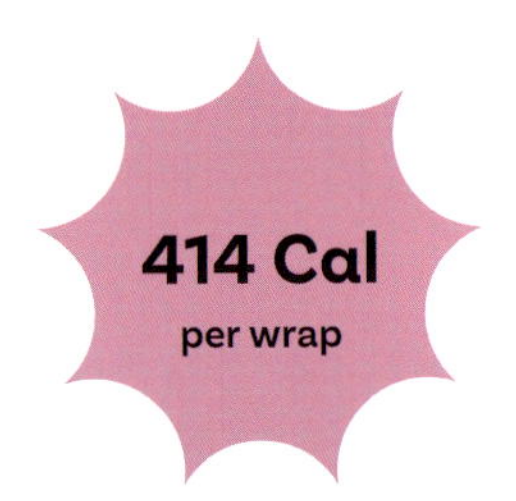

Protein 35.9g | Fat 16.0g | Carbs 35.7g

MAKES 1
TAKES 20 minutes

Melty on the inside, crispy on the outside, this breakfast wrap is such an easy recipe to throw together for a delicious start to the day. Sausages and hash browns are a good alternative if you fancy switching things up.

Ingredients

2 bacon medallions

Low calorie cooking spray

2 eggs, beaten

1 tortilla wrap

Handful of spinach

1 tomato, sliced

10g reduced sugar tomato ketchup

15g reduced fat Cheddar, grated

Method

- Preheat the grill to medium. Grill the bacon medallions for 7 minutes until crispy.
- While the bacon is cooking, spray a medium frying pan with low calorie cooking spray. Over a medium heat, add the eggs, ensuring the surface of the pan is covered.
- Once the eggs start to set, place the wrap over the top. Flip carefully and remove from the pan.
- Slice halfway down the wrap in the middle. In the first quarter, add the bacon, in the second add the spinach, in the third the sliced tomato and the tomato ketchup and in the final quarter the cheese.
- Fold each quarter over itself.
- In a frying pan over a low heat, pan-fry the wrap, cheese-side down, for 3–4 minutes until melted.

Cheesy Hash Brown Bake

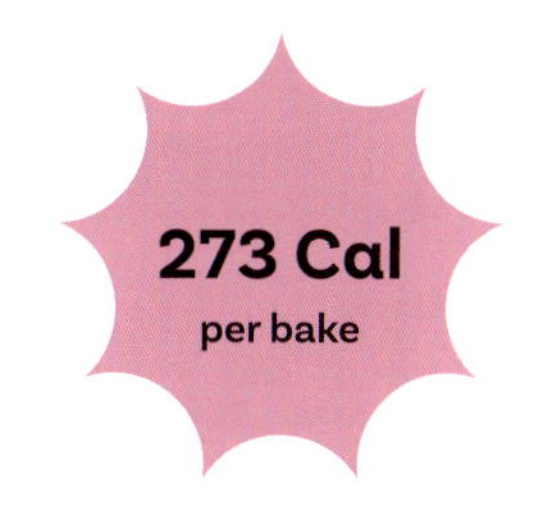

Protein 24.5g | Fat 13.0g | Carbs 14.5g

SERVES 2
TAKES 35 minutes

Hash browns are the ultimate breakfast food – there is nothing they cannot do. Each bite of this bake is super satisfying. Larger hash browns work best here, but if you can only find the smaller ones, then double up to create more of a potato base. Adapt the recipe to whatever meat suits you best, and you can even meal prep this ahead of time for a breezier start to your day.

Ingredients

2 frozen hash browns

Low calorie cooking spray

80g lean bacon, diced

2 medium eggs

100ml skimmed milk

Handful of spinach, chopped

2 tbsp chopped tomatoes

25g reduced fat Cheddar, grated

Salt and pepper

Method

- Preheat the oven to 180°C/160°C fan.
- Lightly toast the hash browns in the toaster for a couple of minutes. Meanwhile, spray a frying pan with low calorie cooking spray, add the bacon and cook over a medium heat for 7 minutes.
- In a jug, mix together the eggs, milk and spinach and season with salt and pepper.
- Grab 2 single-serve ovenproof dishes, then add the hash brown patties and pour over the egg mixture in the jug.
- On the centre of each hash brown, add 1 tablespoon of chopped tomatoes. Top with the bacon and the cheese. Bake in the oven for 20–25 minutes or until golden on top.
- To reheat, simply pop in the microwave for a couple of minutes until piping throughout.

Chocolate French Toast Stack

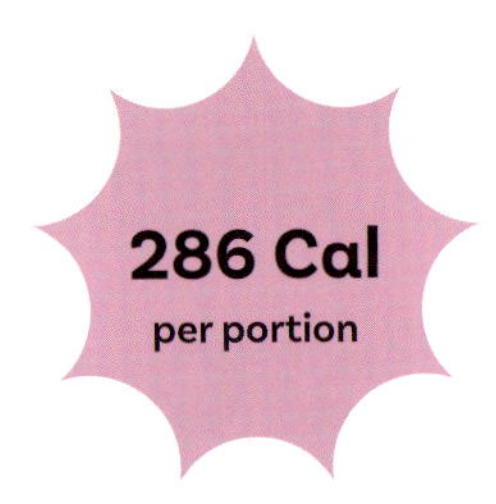

Protein 11.8g | Fat 5.7g | Carbs 48.4g

SERVES 1
TAKES 20 minutes

This chocolate-stuffed French toast stack is seriously good. Crispy, golden, chocolate-filled sticks piled high with strawberries and more chocolate. Any sweet-toothed breakfast goers, this one's for you. You can add a scoop of chocolate protein powder in place of the cocoa powder if you wish. Preferably use bread that is a little stale so it holds up better in the batter. If you can't find no-crust bread, any low calorie bread will do.

Ingredients

1 egg, beaten

80ml almond milk

1 tsp cocoa powder

15g low calorie chocolate spread (I use Sweet Freedom Choc Pot)

4 slices of no-crust white bread

Low calorie cooking spray

Handful of strawberries, sliced

5g low calorie chocolate drizzle

¼ tsp icing sugar

Method

- Mix together the egg, milk and cocoa powder in a shallow bowl and set to one side.
- Spread the chocolate spread onto 2 slices of the bread, top with the remaining slices of bread, then slice into sticks. Dip each sandwiched stick into the batter but be careful not to soak for too long.
- While you are dipping the sticks, place a frying pan over a medium heat and lightly spray with low calorie cooking spray. Once hot, fry each stick for 3–4 minutes on each side until golden.
- Once cooked, stack your French toast sticks on top of each other, adding sliced strawberries between each layer. Top with more strawberries, the chocolate drizzle and icing sugar.
- **Air fryer** – Once you have completed step 2, pop your sticks in the air fryer (either straight into the drawer, or use a silicone liner to minimise mess). Cook at 175°C for 7–8 minutes. Then assemble as explained in step 4.

No-bake Choc Chip Granola Bars

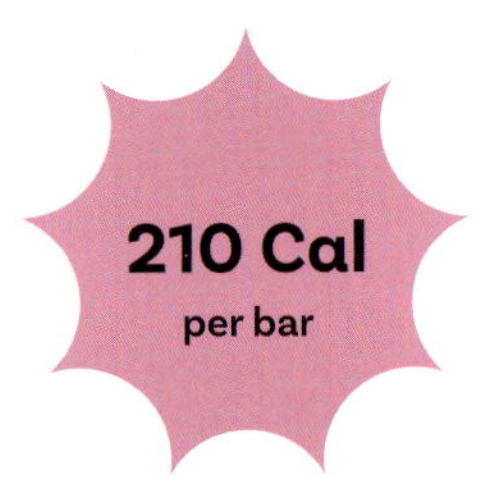

Protein 5.6g | Fat 8.0g | Carbs 27.0g

MAKES 8

TAKES 15 minutes, plus 1 hour+ chilling

Super easy with no hidden nasty ingredients, plus these bars are a lot bigger than the ones you buy from the shop! I love to pair these with a yoghurt bowl and some fruit but they are also a perfect on-the-go breakfast when wrapped individually. If you're feeling extra cheeky, drizzle over some melted dark chocolate and flaked sea salt.

Ingredients

100g rolled oats

50g rice puff cereal

1 tsp sea salt

30g chocolate chips of your choice, chopped

100g smooth peanut butter

100g runny honey

1 tsp vanilla extract

Method

- Line a 20cm square baking tin with baking paper, ensuring there is some overhanging the edges.
- In a bowl, combine the oats, rice puff cereal, sea salt and chopped chocolate chips.
- In a saucepan over a medium heat, add the peanut butter, honey and vanilla extract. Whisk until combined.
- Pour the wet mixture into the dry ingredients. Continue to mix until all the ingredients are combined.
- Transfer the mixture to the prepared tin. Press down and fill the tin with the back of a spoon. To ensure the mixture fully sets, use your hands to press down further.
- Chill in the fridge for at least 1 hour. Remove from the tin and slice into 8 bars. Store in an airtight container, layered with baking paper to prevent sticking, for up to a week. If you plan on enjoying these bars on the go, wrap them individually in baking paper using a little sticky tape to keep them in the paper.

Molten Chocolate Baked Oats

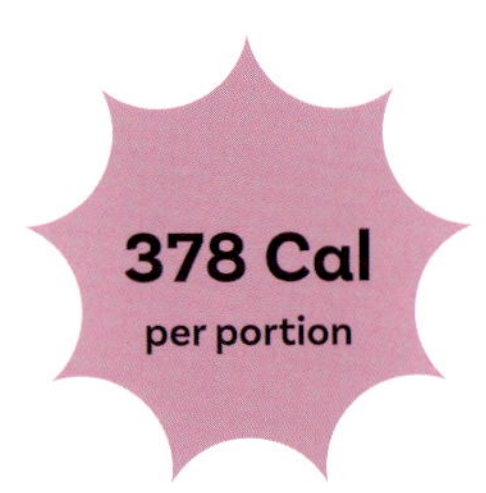

Protein 16.4g | Fat 14.6g | Carbs 45.3g

SERVES 1
TAKES 30 minutes

The baked oats craze isn't ending over here. With their perfect cake-like texture and melting chocolate middle, hitting your goals at breakfast has never been easier. Pair with some fruit on top.

Ingredients

50g rolled oats
1 tsp cocoa powder
½ tsp baking powder
¼ tsp salt
1 tbsp granulated sweetener
1 medium egg
50ml skimmed milk
½ tsp vanilla extract
Low calorie cooking spray
1 square of dark chocolate, frozen slightly
5g milk chocolate chips

Method

- Preheat the oven to 180°C/160°C fan.
- For a smooth cake-like texture, place the oats, cocoa powder, baking powder, salt, sweetener, egg, skimmed milk and vanilla extract in a blender and blast for 20 seconds until smooth. If you do not have a blender, you can mix the ingredients in a mixing bowl.
- Spray a small ramekin dish with low calorie cooking spray before pouring in the batter. Press the dark chocolate into the centre of the batter, ensuring it is covered.
- Top with the chocolate chips, then bake in the oven for 20 minutes. The oats are ready when a toothpick inserted into the centre comes out clean. Leave to cool slightly before devouring!

Oven-baked Pancake Bites

Protein 3.3g | Fat 15.0g | Carbs 9.4g

MAKES 10

TAKES 20 minutes

Who doesn't love a pancake? Making ahead and baking in the oven means you can still have them during the morning rush to get out the door. Perfect on their own, or pair them with a yoghurt bowl. And why not switch them up to whatever fruit and chocolate suits your taste buds?!

Ingredients

Low calorie cooking spray (optional)

110g self-raising flour

3 tbsp granulated sweetener

¼ tsp salt

½ tsp bicarbonate of soda

2 medium eggs

1 tsp vanilla extract

1 tsp lemon juice

50g fat-free Greek yoghurt

120ml skimmed milk

50g frozen raspberries, crushed

10g white chocolate drops

Method

- Preheat the oven to 180°C/160°C fan and line a 12-hole muffin tray with 10 silicone moulds. Alternatively, spray 10 muffin holes with low calorie cooking spray.
- Mix together the flour, sweetener, salt and bicarbonate of soda in a mixing jug.
- Crack in the eggs and whisk them into the dry ingredients, then add the vanilla extract, lemon juice, yoghurt and milk. Stir until completely combined. You can also do this into a blender for a smoother batter.
- Fill the moulds (or holes) two-thirds of the way to the top. Divide the raspberries and chocolate drops evenly between the bites.
- Bake in the oven for 12 minutes. The bites are cooked when a toothpick inserted into the centre comes out clean.

These bites last in the fridge for up to 3 days. Alternatively, freeze the batter in an ice-cube tray and pop into silicone moulds when you're ready to cook.

Loaded Strawberry Overnight Oats

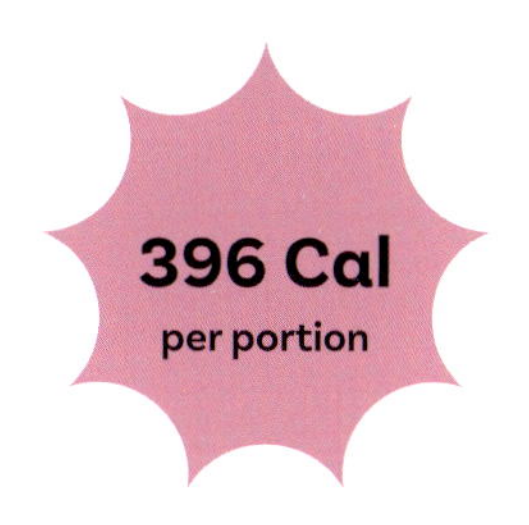

Protein 22.6g | **Fat 5.8g** | **Carbs 59.8g**

SERVES 1

TAKES 10 minutes, plus 4 hours+ chilling

Fresh summery flavours prepped for an easy start to the day. Layers of strawberries, creamy oats, yoghurt, jam and crumbled biscuit make this a breakfast to die for. For an added protein boost, stir through a scoop of vanilla protein powder.

Ingredients

40g rolled oats

180g strawberry Icelandic-style yoghurt

40ml almond milk (or any other skimmed milk)

1 tsp vanilla extract

1 tsp granulated sweetener

100g strawberries, chopped into small pieces

10g digestive biscuit

1 tsp strawberry jam

Method

- In a bowl, mix together the oats, 150g of the yoghurt, the milk, vanilla extract and sweetener.
- Add half of the strawberries to the bottom of a small glass jar, then top with the oat mixture. Top with a quarter of the strawberries, then add the remaining 30g of yoghurt.
- Crumble over half the biscuit, add the dollop of jam in the centre, then finish with the remaining biscuit and strawberries.
- Place in the fridge for at least 4 hours, or ideally overnight. These oats can be kept in the fridge for 3 days.

Two

LUNCHES TO LOOK FORWARD TO

Pizza-flavoured Prep Bowls

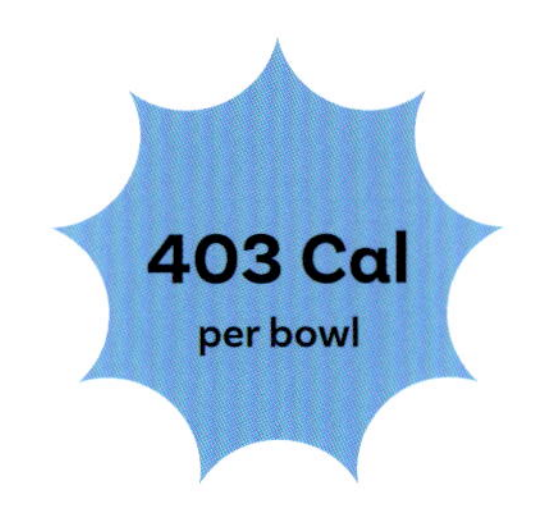

Protein 42.0g | **Fat 17.0g** | **Carbs 15.0g**

MAKES 2
TAKES 35 minutes

When those lunchtime cravings for pizza hit, then these prepped bowls have got you covered and won't leave you feeling sluggish afterwards. Loaded with veggies and protein, these bowls will keep you feeling full until dinner time. Customise using turkey or chicken mince, or swap the fillings for your favourite pizza toppings.

Ingredients

Low calorie cooking spray
1 tsp garlic purée
1 red onion, diced
200g lean beef mince
1 green pepper, diced
140g mushrooms, sliced
1 tbsp tomato purée
1¼ tsp Italian herb seasoning
30g mozzarella, grated
30g pepperoni, sliced
30g reduced fat Cheddar, grated
basil leaves, to garnish

Tomato sauce

200g passata
1 tsp garlic granules
1 tsp Italian herb seasoning
1 tsp sweetener
Salt and pepper

Method

- Spray a frying pan with low calorie cooking spray. Over a medium heat, add the garlic purée and red onion and fry for 3-4 minutes until fragrant. Add the beef mince and continue to cook until it is brown.
- While the beef is cooking, in a bowl mix together all the sauce ingredients. Leave to one side.
- Preheat the oven to 180°C/160°C fan.
- Once the beef has browned, add the green pepper and mushrooms to the pan and cook for 3-4 minutes until they have softened. Add the tomato purée and 1 teaspoon of the Italian herb seasoning and cook for a further minute. Stir through half of the tomato sauce and take off the heat.
- In two circular ovenproof dishes, add the beef mixture, then top with the remaining tomato sauce.
- Add the grated mozzarella and the pepperoni, followed by the grated Cheddar. Sprinkle over the remaining ¼ teaspoon of Italian herb seasoning and bake in the oven for 15-20 minutes until golden.
- Garnish with basil leaves and leave to cool slightly before eating. If prepping ahead of time, allow it to cool completely before refrigerating; make sure to cover with a lid. When ready to eat, heat on high in the microwave for a couple of minutes until piping hot

Hot Caesar Chicken Tacos

Protein 48.8g | Fat 11.5g | Carbs 37.3g

SERVES 2
TAKES 30 minutes

I think most of us can agree that Caesar salad is delicious... but wrapped in tacos with added sriracha sauce, this is a combination to die for. If you want to use store-bought light Caesar dressing, then use that and just add the teaspoon of sriracha sauce listed.

Ingredients

200g chicken breast
1 tsp garlic granules
1 tsp onion granules
4 bacon medallions
4 mini tortilla wraps
1 head of romaine lettuce, chopped
15g Parmesan, grated
Salt and pepper

Caesar sauce

40g lighter than light mayonnaise
1 tbsp fat-free Greek yoghurt
1 tsp Worcestershire sauce
1 tsp lemon juice
1 tsp sriracha sauce
¼ tsp garlic granules
½ tsp Dijon mustard
1 tsp white wine vinegar

Method

- Preheat the oven to 180°C/160°C fan.
- In a bowl, season the chicken with the garlic granules, onion granules, and salt and pepper to taste. Place on a baking tray and cook in the centre of the oven for 18 minutes. Once cooked, shred using 2 forks.
- Meanwhile, combine all the ingredients for the Caesar sauce in a bowl, season and set to one side. Preheat the grill to high.
- While the chicken is still cooking, grill the bacon for 7 minutes. Once cooked, cut into small square pieces.
- Slightly warm the tortilla wraps in the microwave for 10–15 seconds. Add the Caesar sauce along the bottom, and top with the chicken, lettuce, bacon and Parmesan. Fold in half and place in a frying pan over a medium heat, sauce-side down, for 1½ minutes. Top with another frying pan or heavy heatproof bowl to help keep them closed. Do not flip them, as this helps to maintain a crunch in the lettuce.

Chopped Ranch Salad Sandwich

Protein 40.5g | Fat 10.0g | Carbs 35.0g

MAKES 1
TAKES 25 minutes

Chopping all of the ingredients on top of each other ensures a delicious, flavoursome bite every time. Use pre-cooked chicken and store-bought ranch sauce for a speedier lunch option.

Ingredients

100g chicken breast
½ tsp garlic granules
½ tsp onion granules
¼ tsp dried parsley
¼ tsp dried dill
¼ tsp dried chives
1 unsmoked bacon rasher
1 deli sub roll
Handful of shredded lettuce
1 salad tomato, sliced
Salt and pepper

Ranch sauce

20g lighter than light mayonnaise
1 tbsp fat-free natural yoghurt
½ tsp garlic granules
¼ tsp onion granules
¼ tsp dried parsley
⅛ tsp dried dill
¼ tsp dried chives

Method

- Preheat the oven to 180°C/160°C fan.
- Season the chicken breast with the garlic granules, onion granules, parsley, dill, chives and some salt and pepper. Rub the seasonings into the chicken breast thoroughly. Transfer to a baking tray and bake in the oven for 16 minutes.
- Mix together all the ingredients for the ranch sauce and set to one side.
- Preheat the grill to high.
- Place the bacon under the grill and cook until crispy on both sides.
- Lightly toast the sub roll under the grill until lightly browned.
- On a chopping board, place the lettuce, the cooked chicken and bacon and the sliced tomato. If using pre-cooked chicken, season with salt and pepper.
- Using a sharp knife, carefully chop everything together into smaller pieces.
- Add the ranch sauce on top, then chop one last time before scooping up all the ingredients into the toasted roll.

Creamy Sweet Chilli Pasta Salad Jar

Protein 40.0g | **Fat 3.7g** | **Carbs 59.2g**

SERVES 1
TAKES 20 minutes

This is your answer to those soggy pasta salad nightmares once you're at work. By layering the salad with the sauce at the bottom, the salad remains intact until you pour it all out into a bowl. You can change the lettuce to any leaves you prefer and even add some grated cheese if you fancy it.

Ingredients

100g chicken breast, diced
¾ tsp smoked paprika
½ tsp garlic granules
½ tsp chilli paste
Low calorie cooking spray
50g dried short pasta (I use rigatoni)
15g lighter than light mayonnaise
25g reduced sugar sweet chilli sauce
50g fat-free Greek yoghurt
1 tbsp white wine vinegar
1 small red pepper, diced
1 small red onion, diced
50g shredded lettuce
Salt

Method

- In a bowl, season the chicken with ½ teaspoon of the smoked paprika, the garlic granules, ¼ teaspoon of the chilli paste and some salt and mix well.
- Spray a frying pan with low calorie cooking spray, add the chicken and fry over a medium-high heat for 10 minutes until cooked through. Remove from the heat.
- Cook the pasta in a pan of boiling salted water according to the packet instructions.
- Meanwhile, mix together the mayo, sweet chilli sauce, yoghurt, vinegar, remaining ¼ teaspoon of smoked paprika and ¼ teaspoon of chilli paste in a bowl. Add 2–3 tablespoons of pasta water and mix until a thinner smooth sauce has formed.
- Drain the pasta and rinse in cold water to prevent further cooking. Allow to cool slightly.
- Take a 600–800ml Mason jar and add the sauce to the bottom, followed by the cooked chicken, pasta, diced red pepper and red onion and the shredded lettuce.
- Store in the fridge for 2–3 days. When serving, empty the jar into a bowl and mix the ingredients together.

Crispy Potato Salad

Protein 14.3g | Fat 7.2g | Carbs 69.2g

SERVES 1

TAKES 50 minutes

Once you go crispy, there is no going back. Crispy potatoes hold up so much better in a potato salad recipe, and the best part about this recipe? It's best made ahead so the flavours develop in the fridge. If you add meat, eggs or a veggie alternative to serve alongside, this recipe can feed two people. Best served with leafy greens for a complete lunch.

Ingredients

400g baby potatoes

Olive oil spray

50g fat-free Greek yoghurt

50g lighter than light mayonnaise

1 tbsp lemon juice

¼ tsp Dijon mustard

1 tsp garlic powder

1 tsp onion powder

1 tbsp fresh dill, chopped

1 tbsp fresh parsley, chopped

2 spring onions, chopped

10g Red Leicester, grated

Salt and pepper

Method

- Bring a large pan of salted water to the boil. Add the potatoes and cook for 15 minutes until slightly tender. Drain and leave to steam dry for 5 minutes.
- Preheat the oven to 180°C/160°C fan. Spray a large baking tray with olive oil spray.
- Transfer the potatoes to the baking tray. Using the bottom of a glass, gently press down on the potatoes until they are smashed slightly. Spray with olive oil spray and season with salt and pepper.
- Bake in the oven for 25 minutes until the potatoes are nice and crispy.
- Meanwhile, make the dressing by combining the yoghurt, mayonnaise, lemon juice, mustard, garlic powder, onion powder, dill, parsley and spring onions. Leave to one side until the potatoes are cooked.
- Once the potatoes are cooked, add them to the dressing, tossing well to combine. Stir through the cheese and serve.
- **Air fryer** – Cook the boiled potatoes at 185°C for 20 minutes.

Single Serve Tortilla Bake

Protein 39.9g **Fat 15.0g** **Carbs 41.0g**

MAKES 1
TAKES 25 minutes

Layered crispy tortilla wraps with taco beef mince, enchilada sauce and cheese – this is definitely a lunch recipe you will keep coming back to. It can be prepped ahead of time, lasts a few days in the fridge and can even be reheated so it's as tasty as when it's first pulled out of the oven.

Ingredients

Low calorie cooking spray
2 flour tortilla wraps
100g lean beef mince
½ small white onion, diced
1 tsp garlic purée
1 tsp taco seasoning
½ red pepper, diced
80g enchilada sauce
20g reduced fat Cheddar, grated
1 sprig of fresh coriander, finely chopped

Method

- Preheat the oven to 180°C/160°C fan.
- Spray a frying pan with low calorie cooking spray. Once the pan is hot, add the tortilla wraps. Fry on each side for a minute or two until slightly crisp. Wraps usually form bubbles when they are ready to be flipped. Remove from the pan.
- Add the beef mince and onion to the pan and fry for 5–7 minutes until the beef is almost brown. Then add the garlic purée, taco seasoning and red pepper. Sauté for another couple of minutes.
- In a small circular ovenproof dish or a dish you can take on the go, add 20g of the enchilada sauce, followed by the first tortilla, and push in carefully to create a pie-like shape.
- Top with half the meat mixture, another 20g enchilada sauce and half of the cheese, followed by the next tortilla.
- Repeat with the remaining meat mixture, enchilada sauce and cheese.
- Bake in the oven for 15 minutes. Finish with chopped coriander.

Tuna Garlic Bread Melt

Protein 45.1g | **Fat 11.3g** | **Carbs 47.4g**

MAKES 1

TAKES 15 minutes

It's no secret that I am partial to a cheeky bit of garlic bread. And, what better way to spruce up a tuna melt than by coating the outsides of the bread with garlic butter, then toasting until beautifully golden? Trust me, once you try it this way there is no going back.

Ingredients

1 tin of tuna in brine, drained (102g drained weight)

¼ small red onion, diced

1 small celery stick, diced

1 tbsp fat-free Greek yoghurt

¼ tsp Dijon mustard

½ tsp lemon juice

10g light butter

½ tsp chopped garlic

½ tsp dried parsley

2 slices of sourdough bread (or other thickly sliced bread)

25g reduced fat Cheddar, grated

Method

- In a bowl, mix together the tuna, red onion, celery, yoghurt, mustard and lemon juice until combined.
- Add the butter, garlic and parsley to a microwavable bowl. Blast in the microwave for 10 seconds and stir until all the ingredients are combined.
- Brush both pieces of bread with the garlic butter. Top one slice with the tuna mixture and the cheese.
- Place the other slice of the bread on top. Transfer to a frying pan over a medium-low heat. Cover and toast for a few minutes on each side until the cheese has melted.

Chipotle Chicken Wraps

Protein 43.5g | **Fat 8.8g** | **Carbs 41.3g**

SERVES 2
TAKES 25 minutes

These wraps were loved by the masses when I first posted them on social media and it is easy to see why. A homemade chipotle lime sauce paired with added crunch and melted cheese? You will be counting down the minutes until lunchtime.

Ingredients

200g chicken breast
1 tsp smoked paprika
1 tsp garlic granules
1 tsp salt
1 tsp lime juice
1 tsp chipotle paste
1 little gem lettuce, chopped
2 tortilla wraps
40g reduced fat Cheddar (or Eatlean cheese), grated
10g chilli tortilla crisps (I use chilli heatwave Doritos)

Sauce

60g lighter than light mayonnaise
60g fat-free Greek yoghurt
1 tsp smoked paprika
1 tsp chipotle paste
1 tbsp lime juice
1 tsp garlic granules
1 tsp dried chives
Pinch of salt

Method

- Preheat the oven to 180°C/160°C fan.
- Season the chicken with the smoked paprika, garlic granules and salt. Rub in thoroughly with your hands. Mix together the lime juice and chipotle paste in a small bowl and brush over the chicken. Place the chicken in an ovenproof dish and cook in the oven for 20 minutes.
- While the chicken is cooking, mix together all the ingredients for the sauce with 1 tablespoon of water. Once combined, stir through the lettuce, ensuring it is all coated in the sauce.
- Lightly warm each tortilla wrap in the microwave for 15 seconds.
- Once the chicken is cooked, chop the chicken into bite-sized pieces. Line each tortilla with the lettuce, the chicken, the cheese and the crisps (you may need to crush the crisps to make folding easier).
- Start to roll by tucking the wrap under, folding the sides as you go to form a burrito shape.
- Over a medium heat, lightly pan-fry the wraps for 3–4 minutes until golden. (Feel free to skip this step if you don't like warm lettuce.)
- **Air fryer** – Cook the coated chicken at 180°C for 17 minutes.

Red Thai Chicken Curry Fried Rice

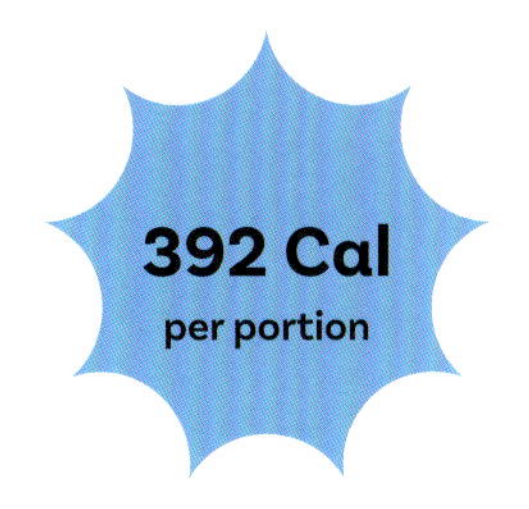

Protein 34.4g | **Fat 5.7g** | **Carbs 49.6g**

SERVES 2

TAKES 25 minutes

Red Thai curries are a favourite from my backpacking years. I wanted to create a similar taste, but in a lunch-friendly form, and this is where fried rice comes into play. Fragrant, comforting and easy to meal prep ahead of time. Add any veggies into this dish – most work well!

Ingredients

250g packet of microwave jasmine rice

Low calorie cooking spray

200g chicken breast, cut into bite-sized pieces

1 small white onion, finely chopped

1 red pepper, finely chopped

1 tsp ginger purée

1 tsp garlic purée

1 tbsp red Thai curry paste

1 tsp fish sauce

1 tbsp lime juice

2 tbsp light coconut milk

1 tbsp light soy sauce

1 spring onion, chopped

Salt and pepper

Method

- Cook the rice according to the packet instructions. Once cooked, leave to one side to cool.
- Spray a frying pan with low calorie cooking spray. Heat over a medium heat and, once hot, add the chicken, season with salt and pepper and fry for 10 minutes until the chicken is almost cooked.
- Once the chicken is almost cooked, add the onion and red pepper and fry for 5 minutes until slightly softened.
- Add the ginger and garlic purées, curry paste, fish sauce and lime juice. Mix well for 2 minutes, then pour in the coconut milk. Stir to combine and then add the rice.
- Make sure the rice is fully combined, then add the soy sauce and mix through.
- Serve topped with the chopped spring onion.

Jalapeño Popper Grilled Cheese

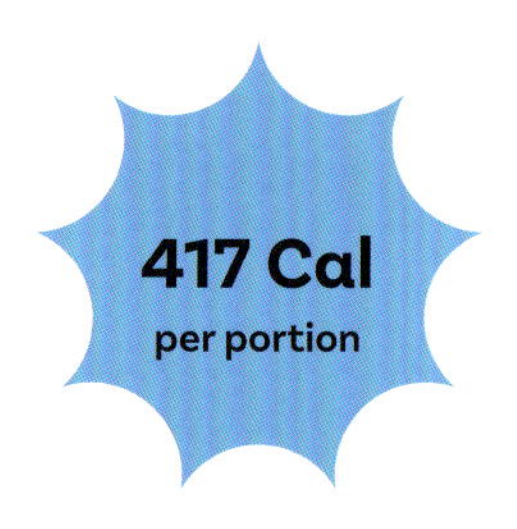

Protein 25.5g | Fat 10.9g | Carbs 52.6g

MAKES 1
TAKES 15 minutes

This grilled cheese is bursting full of flavour with a creamy garlic chive filling laced with diced jalapeños for some heat. The filling also works well on wraps if you want to make lunch ahead of time; just make sure that the wraps are toasted. Lean bacon is a delicious addition for those who wish to add meat.

Ingredients

20g jalapeños from a jar, finely chopped

½ tsp dried chives

½ tsp garlic granules

50g light cream cheese

15g fat-free Greek yoghurt

2 slices of sourdough bread (around 100g)

30g reduced fat Cheddar, grated

Low calorie cooking spray

Salt

Method

- In a bowl, mix together the jalapeños, chives, garlic granules, a pinch of salt, cream cheese and yoghurt.
- Lightly toast the bread. Add the Cheddar cheese and then the creamy jalapeño mixture to one slice and place the other slice on top.
- Spray a frying pan with low calorie cooking spray and add the sandwich. Leave the sandwich over a medium heat, covered, for a few minutes. Then spray with low calorie spray and flip onto the other side, cover and cook for a further few minutes.

Creamy Peri Peri Pitta

Protein 40.9g | **Fat 8.8g** | **Carbs 31.0g**

SERVES 1
TAKES 25 minutes

I have been hooked on making creamy pitta bread variations for a while now. But this peri version has got to be the best yet. If you're making it ahead of time, make sure that the filling is completely cool before wrapping.

Ingredients

100g chicken breast
1 tsp smoked paprika
½ tsp garlic granules
½ tsp onion granules
½ tsp dried oregano
30ml soured cream
20g fat-free Greek yoghurt
1 tbsp peri peri sauce (use a mild one if you don't like spice)
1 pitta bread (I use Warburtons wholemeal soft pitta bread)
¼ round lettuce, sliced
10g chilli jam
1 red onion, diced
2 chives, chopped

Method

- Preheat the oven to 180°C/160°C fan.
- Season the chicken by rubbing in the paprika, garlic granules, onion granules and oregano. Place in an ovenproof dish and bake in the oven for 18 minutes.
- While the chicken is cooking, mix the soured cream, yoghurt and peri peri sauce together in a small bowl.
- Once the chicken is cooked, chop into rough pieces and combine with the peri peri sauce mixture.
- Toast the pitta and add the lettuce, chicken, chilli jam, diced onion and chives.

Cajun Beef Rice

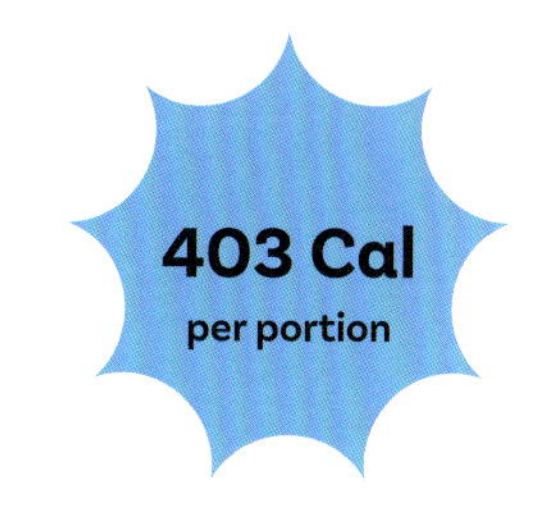

Protein 38.5g | **Fat 8.3g** | **Carbs 41.6g**

SERVES 2
TAKES 25 minutes

Cajun flavours are always a delight, never mind at lunchtime. The rice can be made ahead of time so you never have to go to work without lunch again.

Ingredients

Low calorie cooking spray

1 white onion, diced

2 celery sticks, diced

1 green pepper, diced

1½ tbsp smoky Cajun seasoning (omit the second ½ tbsp if you're sensitive to spice; if you don't have smoky Cajun seasoning, add 1 tsp smoked paprika)

200g lean beef mince

1 tsp garlic purée

2 tbsp tomato purée

1 beef stock cube, crumbled

100ml water

250g packet of microwave Mexican-style rice

30g reduced fat Cheddar (or Eatlean cheese), grated

2 tbsp tomato salsa

Salt and pepper

Salad, to serve

Method

- Heat a frying pan over a medium heat and spray with low calorie cooking spray. Add the onion, celery and green pepper to the pan and cook for a few minutes before adding 1 tablespoon of the Cajun seasoning.
- When the veggies start to soften, add the beef mince and garlic purée and mix well. Cook for a further few minutes.
- Add the remaining Cajun seasoning and tomato purée, season with salt and pepper, then add the crumbled beef stock cube and the water and leave to simmer for 5 minutes.
- Microwave the rice according to the packet instructions, then combine it with the other ingredients in the pan.
- Serve with the grated cheese and tomato salsa and some salad. It will keep in the fridge for up to 3 days.

Croque Monsieur

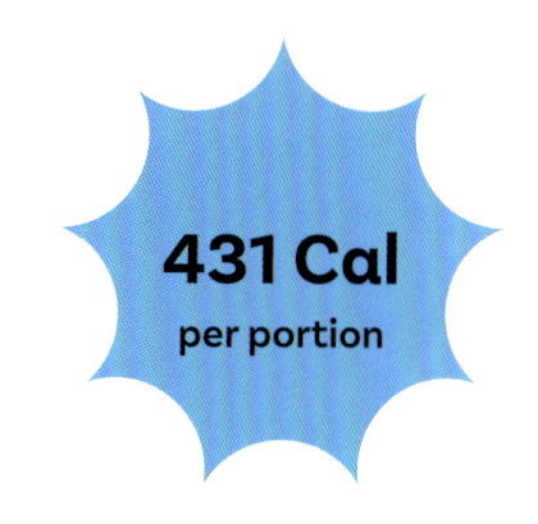

Protein 34.1g | Fat 9.6g | Carbs 50.5g

MAKES 2

TAKES 25 minutes

Hot diggity damn! Toasted bread, creamy sauce, ham and plenty of cheese, this is an effortless lunch that delivers huge flavour for the taste buds.

Ingredients

4 slices of thick bread

100g light creamy white sauce (lasagne sauce)

¼ tsp Dijon mustard

160g sliced ham

50g reduced fat Cheddar, grated

Salt and pepper

Method

- Preheat the oven to 190°C/170°C fan.
- Lightly toast the slices of bread in a toaster.
- In a bowl, mix together the white sauce and mustard and season with salt and pepper to taste.
- Spread each slice of bread with the white sauce mixture. Top 2 of the slices of bread with the ham and half of the cheese, then top with the other bread slices, sauce facing upwards. Finish with the remaining cheese on top of the sauce.
- Place on a baking tray nd bake in the middle of the oven for 12 minutes, or until the cheese is melted, with a golden brown top.
- **Air fryer** – Cook at 180°C for 10 minutes.

Chicken Tinga-style Bowls

Protein 42.4g | **Fat 9.6g** | **Carbs 54.9g**

SERVES 2
TAKES 20 minutes

This used to be my go-to office lunch because not only does it taste good hot, but it also tastes good cold, which is perfect if work microwaves give you the ick. The chicken is seriously tasty and super versatile in wraps or sandwiches if you don't want rice. Prep ahead of time and keep in the fridge for a few days.

Ingredients

200g chicken breast, diced

1 tsp ground cumin

1 tsp smoked paprika

½ tsp dried oregano

Low calorie cooking spray

1 tsp garlic purée

1 white onion, sliced

100ml chicken stock

1 tbsp tomato purée

1 tsp chipotle paste

250g packet of microwave Mexican-style rice

30g reduced fat Cheddar, grated

1 salad tomato, diced

1 red pepper, diced

100g lettuce, shredded

2 sprigs of coriander, chopped

Sauce

40g fat-free Greek yoghurt

1 tbsp lime juice

½ tsp garlic granules

½ tsp chipotle paste

Method

- In a bowl, add the chicken, cumin, smoked paprika and oregano and mix well to combine. Spray a frying pan with low calorie cooking spray and fry the chicken over a medium heat for 10 minutes until cooked through.
- Remove the chicken from the pan and add the garlic purée and sliced onion. While that cooks, shred the chicken using 2 forks.
- Add the chicken stock to a measuring jug and stir through the tomato purée.
- Return the chicken to the pan, add the chicken stock mixture and the chipotle paste (reduce to half the amount if sensitive to spice) and simmer for 5 minutes.
- Mix together all the ingredients for the sauce and set to one side.
- Microwave the rice according to the packet instructions. Divide the rice between 2 bowls and top with the chicken, then the cheese, tomato, red pepper and lettuce. Drizzle over the sauce and garnish with the coriander.
- If prepping ahead of time, I recommend adding the lettuce no more than a day ahead of serving.

Spicy Peanut Noodles

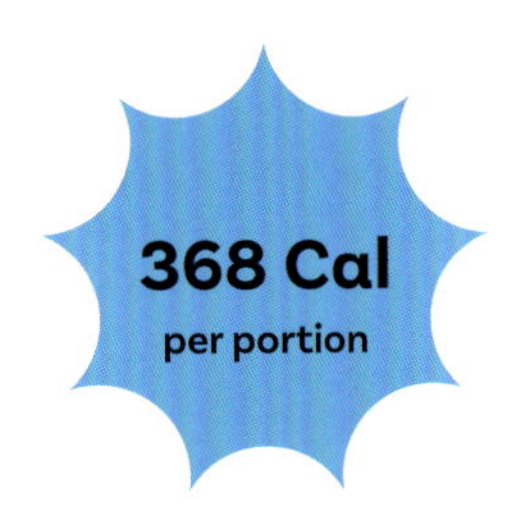

Protein 14.3g | Fat 12.0g | Carbs 60.0g

SERVES 2
TAKES 15 minutes

Ditch those instant noodles and make this quick and easy lunch instead. With layers of creamy peanut butter, saltiness from the soy sauce and a balanced heat from the sriracha, this dish is packed full of flavour. For additional protein, chicken and lean beef mince suit this recipe and, if you have the time, you can throw in some red pepper for added crunch.

Ingredients

2 egg noodle nests
35g smooth peanut butter
1 tbsp light soy sauce
1½ tbsp sriracha sauce
1 tbsp rice wine vinegar
15g runny honey
½ tsp sesame oil
1 tsp ginger purée
1 tsp garlic purée
100ml water
1 tbsp dark soy sauce
2 spring onions, sliced
5g crispy onions
Chilli flakes (optional)

Method

- Add the noodle nests to a pan of boiling water and cook according to the packet instructions.
- In a bowl, mix together the peanut butter, light soy sauce, sriracha, vinegar, honey and 2 tablespoons of boiling water.
- Add the sesame oil to a frying pan over a medium heat, then add the ginger and garlic purées and fry for a minute until fragrant. Add the peanut sauce, followed by the water and stir until the sauce has loosened.
- Add the noodles to the pan, followed by the dark soy sauce. Toss to combine, stirring through half of the spring onions.
- Serve in bowls, garnished with the remaining spring onion, the crispy onions and chilli flakes, if using.

Open Halloumi Bruschetta Toast

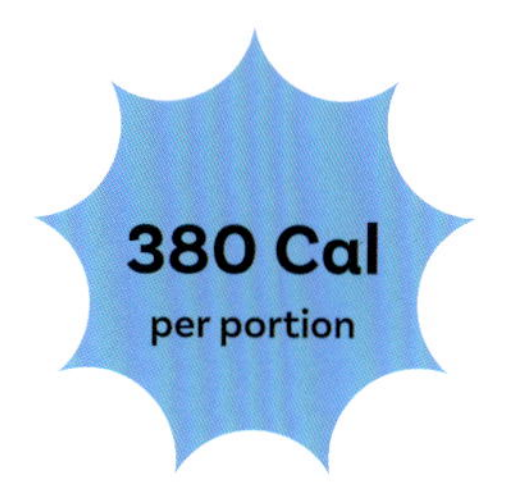

Protein 20.8g | **Fat 9.1g** | **Carbs 51.7g**

SERVES 1
TAKES 20 minutes

Every single bite of this recipe is bursting full of flavour. Adding halloumi on top of the bruschetta adds a depth of salty flavour, which really elevates the dish. A fresh rocket salad drizzled with balsamic glaze would pair wonderfully with this recipe.

Ingredients

100g good-quality cherry tomatoes, quartered

½ tbsp balsamic vinegar

½ tsp garlic purée

¼ tsp dried oregano

3 basil leaves, finely chopped

Low calorie cooking spray

40g reduced fat halloumi, cubed

1 large slice of sourdough bread

Salt

Method

- In a bowl, mix together the tomatoes, vinegar, garlic purée, oregano and basil and season with salt. Leave to one side.
- Spray a frying pan with low calorie cooking spray and add the halloumi. Cook over a medium heat for 3 minutes on each side until golden.
- Spray the slice of sourdough bread with low calorie cooking spray, add it to the pan and cook until it is toasted.
- Top the toasted bread with the tomato mixture and the cooked halloumi.

Three

WEEKNIGHT 'READY MEALS'

Crispy Sweet Chilli Beef Noodles

Protein 39.2g | Fat 7.7g | Carbs 79.8g

SERVES 2
TAKES 25 minutes

Noodles are such a perfect fit for an easy weeknight dinner in a hurry. Made with a sweet and savoury stir-fry sauce, this beef dish is so tasty you will be counting down the hours until dinner time.

Ingredients

2 egg noodle nests
80g Tenderstem broccoli tips
250g beef stir-fry strips
15g cornflour
Olive oil spray
1 white onion, diced
1 red pepper, sliced
1 tsp garlic purée
1 tsp ginger purée
90g reduced sugar sweet chilli sauce
1 tbsp light soy sauce
1 tbsp dark soy sauce
1 tbsp rice wine vinegar
1 tbsp reduced sugar tomato ketchup
1 spring onion, finely diced
Salt and pepper

Method

- Add the noodle nests to a large pan of boiling water and cook for 6–7 minutes. Add the broccoli for 5 minutes to gently cook prior to frying. Drain the noodles and broccoli and rinse the noodles with cold water to prevent them sticking together. Set to one side.
- In a bowl, season the beef with salt and pepper, then add the cornflour, ensuring all of the beef is coated.
- Heat a large frying pan over a high heat and spray with olive oil spray. Once the oil is hot, add the beef strips in a single layer. Leave undisturbed for a couple of minutes before turning. Once the beef is dark brown, remove from the pan and set to one side.
- In the same pan, add the onion, red pepper, broccoli and the garlic and ginger purées and fry for a couple of minutes.
- While the veggies cook, mix together the sweet chilli sauce, light soy sauce, dark soy sauce, vinegar and ketchup. Pour half of the mixture into the frying pan, along with the cooked beef. Coat well in the sauce before adding the noodles and remaining sauce.
- Toss well so that all of the ingredients are combined. Serve immediately with the spring onion scattered over the top.
- **Air fryer** – Add 1 egg white to the same bowl as the beef, cornflour and seasoning and mix well. Cook the beef at 195°C for 12 minutes, shaking throughout. Add to the cooked noodles and vegetables as above.

Garlic Chicken Bacon Parm Tacos

Protein 50.7g | Fat 19.0g | Carbs 33.0g

SERVES 2/**MAKES** 4 tacos
TAKES under 20 minutes

Perfect for taco Tuesdays, these tacos are filled with a creamy garlic herb chicken mix, bacon and cheese. Sub the streaky rashers for bacon medallions if you want a lighter bite.

Ingredients

200g chicken breast
1 tsp garlic granules
1 tsp onion granules
1 tsp dried oregano
Low calorie cooking spray
1 white onion, diced
1 tsp garlic purée
4 streaky bacon rashers (you can substitute for medallions for a lighter option)
1 chicken stock cube, crumbled
45g 50% less fat garlic cream cheese
100ml water
4 mini tortilla wraps
2 reduced fat mature Cheddar slices, halved
10g Parmesan, grated
Dried parsley
Salt and pepper

Method

- Season the chicken with the garlic and onion granules, oregano, and salt and pepper to taste. Rub in thoroughly. Preheat the grill to medium.
- Spray a frying pan with low calorie cooking spray and set over a medium heat. Once hot, add the onion and garlic purée. Sauté for a couple of minutes, then add the chicken.
- While the chicken is cooking, grill the bacon for 7 minutes.
- When the chicken is almost cooked, shred it in the pan with 2 forks. Add the crumbled stock cube, cream cheese and water.
- Add a slice of cooked bacon to each tortilla. Top with the halved slices of cheese and the chicken mixture, then finish with the Parmesan and a sprinkle of parsley.
- Pan-fry in a clean frying pan over a medium heat for 3 minutes on each side until golden and the cheese has melted.

One-pan Creamy Chicken Lasagne

Protein 51.6g | **Fat 14.9g** | **Carbs 43.5g**

SERVES 2

TAKES 30 minutes

Usually we opt for tomato-based lasagnes, but creamy ones are just as delicious. Here I have used chicken and bacon with ranch-style seasonings for the most addictive dinner.

Ingredients

40g lean bacon, diced

200g chicken breast, diced

1 tsp garlic purée

300ml chicken stock

200g light white pasta sauce

30g lightest soft cream cheese

1½ tsp garlic granules

1 tsp onion granules

¼ tsp dried dill

1 tsp dried parsley

1 tsp dried chives

85g dried lasagne sheets, broken in half

50g reduced fat Cheddar, grated

A few sprigs of fresh parsley, chopped

Salt and pepper

Method

- Start by frying the diced bacon in a large frying pan over a high heat for 4–5 minutes. Once cooked, remove from the pan.
- In the same pan, add the chicken and season with salt and pepper. Continue to fry for 12 minutes until the chicken is cooked, then add the garlic purée and cook for a further minute.
- Add the chicken stock, white sauce, cream cheese and the seasonings, along with some salt and pepper, and mix well. Add the lasagne sheets, ensuring they are fully submerged under the liquid. Leave over a medium heat for 10 minutes.
- Once the lasagne sheets are cooked through, give it all a stir before topping with the cheese and the cooked bacon. Cover for a few minutes until the cheese has melted through, then garnish with the fresh parsley.

If you want a crispy top, pop under the grill for a couple of minutes.

Hunter's Sausage Traybake

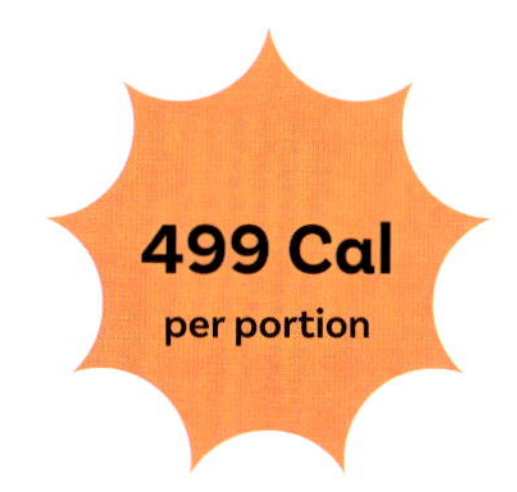

Protein 28.5g | **Fat 19.0g** | **Carbs 51.2g**

SERVES 2
TAKES 30 minutes

This recipe takes me back to my uni days. My mum and I would always have hunter's chicken when I would visit and it is still one of my favourite recipes. Sausage elevates the barbecue flavours but feel free to swap them for chicken or turkey sausages for a higher protein version!

Ingredients

4 low-fat sausages
4 rashers of streaky bacon
160g frozen sweet potato chunks
1 red onion, sliced
1 red pepper, sliced
½ tsp barbecue seasoning
Low calorie cooking spray
40g barbecue sauce
40g reduced fat Cheddar, grated
Salt and pepper
Salad, to serve

Method

- Preheat the oven to 180°C/160°C fan.
- Wrap each sausage in a piece of bacon. Place in a large casserole dish or baking tray. Add the sweet potato, red onion and red pepper, arranging them around the sausages.
- Season all over with salt, pepper and the barbecue seasoning and then spray with low calorie cooking spray. Cook, uncovered, on the middle shelf of the oven for 20 minutes.
- Once the time is up, pour the barbecue sauce over the sausages and sprinkle over the cheese. Return to the oven for a further 5 minutes.
- Serve with a side salad.

Coconut Tandoori Chicken

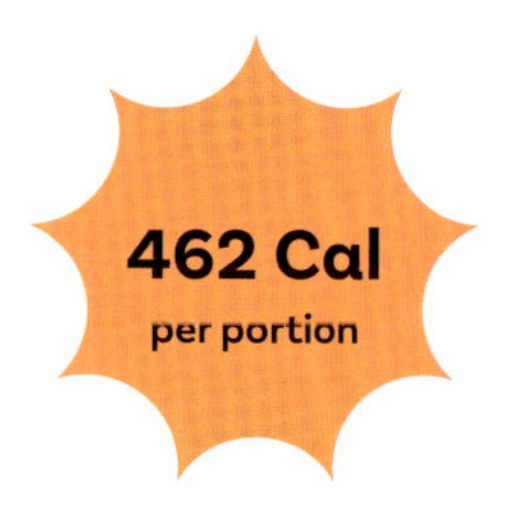

Protein 33.8g **Fat 18.0g** **Carbs 42.0g**

SERVES 2
TAKES 25 minutes

I think this has to be one of my favourite recipes for an easy weeknight dinner. I could devour it straight out of the pan. If you want to add some veggies, peppers and diced courgette pair deliciously with the creamy sauce.

Ingredients

1½ tsp smoked paprika
½ tsp ground coriander
½ tsp ground cumin
½ tsp garlic powder
½ tsp onion powder
½ tsp ground fenugreek
½ tsp ground ginger
1 tsp garam masala
200g chicken breast, diced
200ml coconut milk
Low calorie cooking spray
1 tsp tomato purée
1 tsp granulated sweetener
Handful of spinach
250g packet of microwave pilau rice
3 sprigs of fresh coriander, finely chopped
Salt and pepper

Method

- To make the spice blend, mix all the spices together in a bowl. Use half of this spice blend to coat the chicken. Rub in thoroughly, using your hands, then add 30ml of the coconut milk, stirring to combine. Cover, and leave to marinate in the fridge for as long as possible, although if you're short on time, even 10 minutes will do!
- Spray a medium frying pan with low calorie cooking spray and, over a medium heat, add the chicken and fry for 10–12 minutes until almost cooked through.
- Add the tomato purée, the remaining coconut milk, remaining spice blend and the sweetener to the pan. Give it a good stir before adding the spinach. Leave to simmer over a medium heat for 15 minutes until thickened.
- Cook the rice according to the packet instructions.
- Serve the chicken over the rice, scattered with the coriander.

Full-fat coconut milk gives this recipe maximum flavour. Not all coconut milks have the same calorie and fat content, so make sure to check those labels for the one best-suited to you.

Sticky Teriyaki Beef and Rice

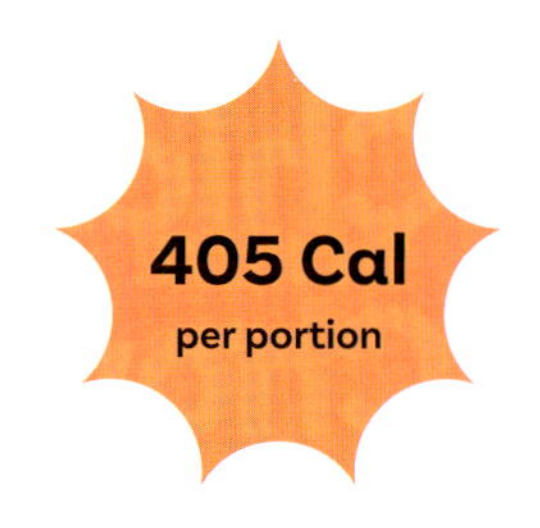

Protein 31.5g | Fat 6.8g | Carbs 52.7g

SERVES 2
TAKES 20 minutes

Teriyaki is usually made with chicken but it is just as banging with beef. A deceptively easy dish, which is perfect for a midweek meal.

Ingredients

Low calorie cooking spray
200g lean beef mince
1 carrot, peeled and cut into matchsticks
1 small red pepper, sliced
250g packet of microwave long-grain rice
1 spring onion, finely chopped

Teriyaki sauce

3 tbsp light soy sauce
1 tbsp dark soy sauce
2 tbsp rice wine vinegar
20g runny honey
1 tsp light brown sugar
1 tsp ginger purée
1 tsp garlic purée
2 tbsp water

Method

- Mix together all the ingredients for the sauce and set to one side.
- Spray a frying pan with low calorie cooking spray. Add the beef mince, breaking it into small pieces using a spatula, and cook over a medium-high heat for 5 minutes until almost browned.
- Add the carrot and red pepper and continue to cook until the beef is completely cooked through. Turn down the heat and add the teriyaki sauce. Mix the sauce in well so that the beef is completely coated.
- Cook the rice according to the packet instructions.
- Serve the beef over the rice, garnishing with the spring onion.

Baked Creamy Cajun Beef Wraps

Protein 48.6g | Fat 10.0g | Carbs 58.3g

SERVES 2

TAKES 20–25 minutes

Buckle up because these bad boys are delicious. A super quick filling made with Cajun seasoning, wrapped up in a tortilla, topped with nacho cheese dip and cheese before being baked for that ultimate bite.

Ingredients

Low calorie cooking spray

200g lean beef mince

1 tsp garlic purée

1 red pepper, diced

1 red onion, diced

1 tbsp Cajun seasoning

1 tsp smoked paprika

2 tbsp salsa

60g extra light cream cheese

50ml water

4 low calorie wraps (I use Weight Watchers wraps)

30g nacho cheese dipping sauce (you can substitute for salsa for a lighter option)

50g reduced fat Cheddar (or Eatlean cheese), grated

a few sprigs of fresh coriander

Salt

Method

- Preheat the oven to 180°C/160°C fan.
- Spray a large frying pan with low calorie cooking spray and set over a high heat. Once hot, add the beef mince and garlic purée and fry the mince for 10 minutes until almost cooked. Add the pepper and onion along with the Cajun seasoning, smoked paprika and a pinch of salt.
- Fry for a further 2 minutes, then add the salsa, cream cheese and water. Reduce the heat to medium for a couple of minutes, then take the pan off the heat.
- Lightly warm the wraps in the microwave, top with the meat mixture and fold carefully into burrito-style shapes. Transfer to an ovenproof dish, then top with the nacho cheese sauce and grated cheese. Bake in the oven for 10 minutes or until the cheese has melted.
- Scatter over the coriander and enjoy!

Chicken Chow Mein

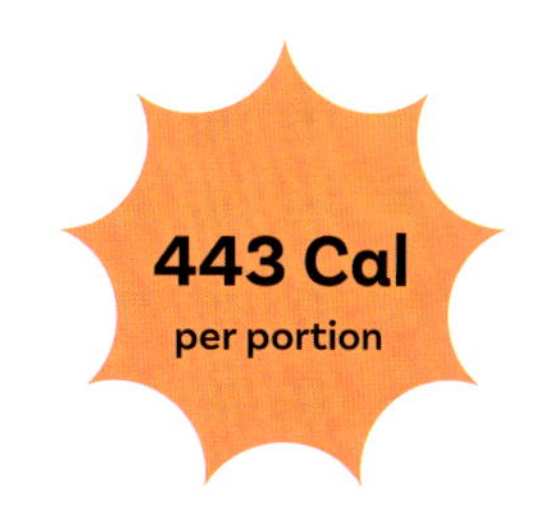

Protein 39.1g | Fat 7.2g | Carbs 65.0g

SERVES 2

TAKES 25 minutes

I think most of us love chicken chow mein and this recipe is much healthier than the takeaway version. If you fancy a change, try pork, or if you're veggie, then swap the chicken for tofu!

Ingredients

1 tbsp light soy sauce

200g chicken, cut into strips

2 egg noodle nests

Low calorie cooking spray

1 tsp garlic purée

150g white cabbage, shredded

1 medium carrot, finely chopped into sticks

1 white onion, sliced

3 spring onions, sliced

100g beansprouts

Sauce

2 tbsp light soy sauce

1 tbsp dark soy sauce

1 tbsp oyster sauce

½ tbsp sweetener (I use granulated)

1 tsp sesame oil

1 tsp rice vinegar

1 tbsp water

Method

- In a bowl, add the 1 tablespoon of soy sauce to the chicken breast and leave to one side.
- Bring a large pan of salted water to the boil and add the noodles. Cook for 4–5 minutes.
- In a bowl, mix together all the ingredients for the sauce and set to one side.
- Spray a wok with low calorie cooking spray, and set over a high heat. Add the chicken and soy sauce mixture and stir-fry for 12–15 minutes until cooked through. Remove from the pan.
- Add the cooked noodles to the wok and leave to char slightly for a couple of minutes. Remove from the wok.
- Add the garlic purée to the empty wok, followed by the white cabbage, carrot, onion and half of the spring onions. Sauté for a few minutes until softened.
- Return the noodles to the wok along with the chicken and beansprouts, then pour in the sauce. Continue cooking for a couple of minutes, ensuring the noodles are fully coated in the sauce.
- Serve immediately with the remaining spring onions to garnish.

Sticky Teriyaki Beef and Rice

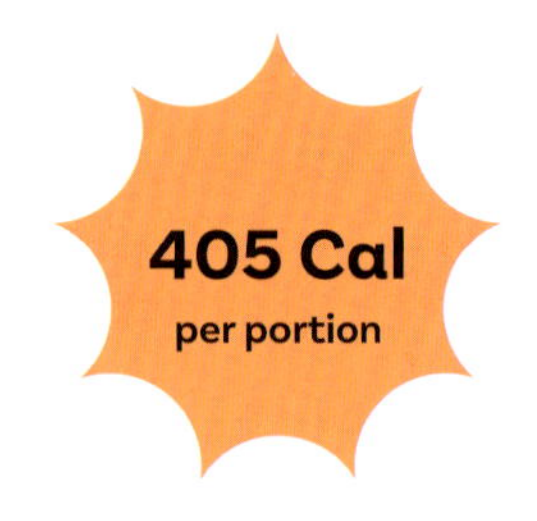

Protein 31.5g | Fat 6.8g | Carbs 52.7g

SERVES 2
TAKES 20 minutes

Teriyaki is usually made with chicken but it is just as banging with beef. A deceptively easy dish, which is perfect for a midweek meal.

Ingredients

Low calorie cooking spray

200g lean beef mince

1 carrot, peeled and cut into matchsticks

1 small red pepper, sliced

250g packet of microwave long-grain rice

1 spring onion, finely chopped

Teriyaki sauce

3 tbsp light soy sauce

1 tbsp dark soy sauce

2 tbsp rice wine vinegar

20g runny honey

1 tsp light brown sugar

1 tsp ginger purée

1 tsp garlic purée

2 tbsp water

Method

- Mix together all the ingredients for the sauce and set to one side.
- Spray a frying pan with low calorie cooking spray. Add the beef mince, breaking it into small pieces using a spatula, and cook over a medium-high heat for 5 minutes until almost browned.
- Add the carrot and red pepper and continue to cook until the beef is completely cooked through. Turn down the heat and add the teriyaki sauce. Mix the sauce in well so that the beef is completely coated.
- Cook the rice according to the packet instructions.
- Serve the beef over the rice, garnishing with the spring onion.

Korean BBQ Beef Quesadillas

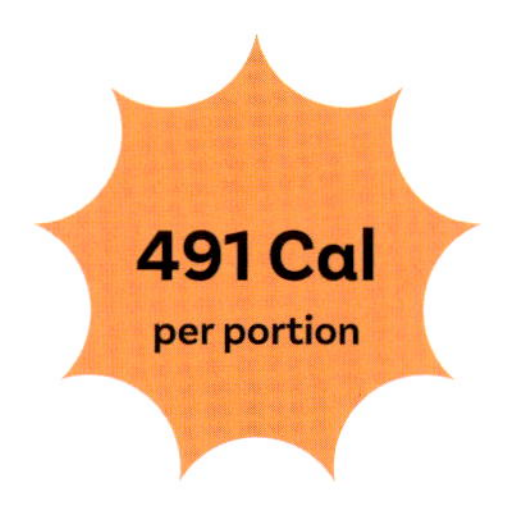

Protein 41.0g | Fat 12.6g | Carbs 51.0g

SERVES 2
TAKES 20 minutes

Gochujang paste has become a staple in my cooking thanks to its peppery chilli taste. Pairing it with barbecue sauce really is a match made in heaven. For my spice lovers, you can add a little bit more paste in this recipe to suit your palate.

Ingredients

Low calorie cooking spray
1 white onion, diced
1 tsp ginger purée
1 tsp garlic purée
200g lean beef mince
1 tbsp light soy sauce
1 tbsp gochujang paste
40g barbecue sauce
1 tbsp hot water
1 medium carrot, grated
2 tortilla wraps
40g reduced fat Cheddar, grated
1½ tsp sriracha mayo
2 spring onions, chopped
lime wedges, to serve

Method

- Spray a frying pan with low calorie cooking spray and set over a medium heat. Once hot, fry the onion, ginger and garlic purées and the beef for 10 minutes until browned.
- Add the soy sauce, gochujang paste, barbecue sauce and water. Combine well, then stir through the grated carrot for a further minute.
- Heat the wraps individually in the microwave for 10 seconds.
- Line each wrap with the cheese and top with the beef, folding into a half-moon shape.
- Spray a clean frying pan with low calorie cooking spray and pan-fry each quesadilla over a medium heat for 3–4 minutes on each side until golden.
- Drizzle over the sriracha mayo and garnish with the chopped spring onions. Serve with lime wedges alongside.

Spinach and Ricotta Pasta Bake

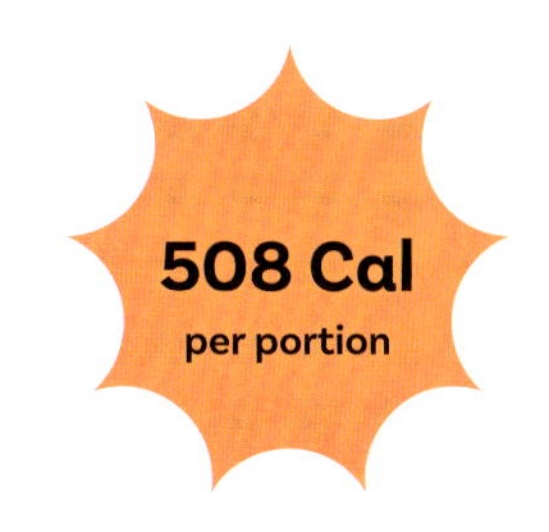

Protein 29.1g | **Fat 15.5g** | **Carbs 60.3g**

SERVES 2
TAKES 35 minutes

Made with a creamy ricotta pasta, topped with a quick tomato sauce and plenty of cheese before being baked until golden, this dish is drool-worthy. You can pack out this bake with courgette, mushrooms or any other veggies if you wish.

Ingredients

120g dried pasta

100g spinach, roughly chopped

250g passata

1 tsp garlic granules

1 tsp Italian herb seasoning

¼ tsp chilli flakes

1 tsp granulated sweetener

250g ricotta

15g Parmesan, grated

40g reduced fat Cheddar, grated

Salt and pepper

Method

- Cook the pasta in a large pan of boiling salted water for 10 minutes. Add the chopped spinach and cook for a further 2 minutes until wilted.
- Meanwhile, in a bowl, mix together the passata, garlic granules, Italian herbs, chilli flakes and sweetener and season with salt and pepper.
- Preheat the oven to 180°C/160°C fan.
- Once the pasta has cooked, reserve 50ml pasta water before draining. Add the ricotta, Parmesan and the pasta water to the pasta and spinach and mix together before transferring to an 18 x 30cm ovenproof dish.
- Top with the tomato mixture, ensuring that the whole surface is covered. Finish by scattering over the Cheddar cheese.
- Bake in the centre of the oven for 20 minutes until the cheese is bubbly and golden.

Hot Honey Halloumi Flatbread

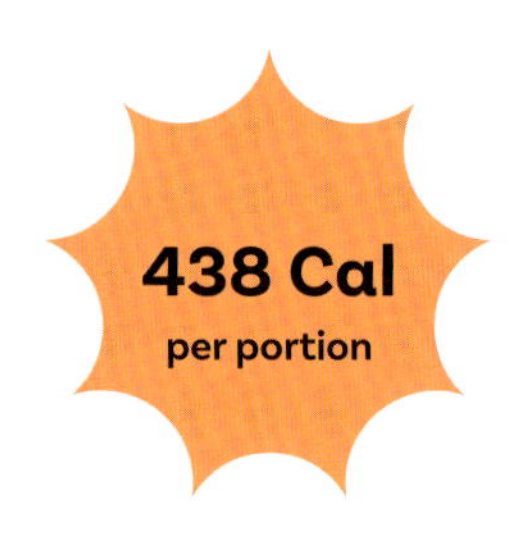

Protein 24.5g | Fat 12.9g | Carbs 52.4g

SERVES 1
TAKES 15 minutes

Ever since hot honey became a thing, I always like to add it to halloumi where I can. Layered on top of soft flatbreads, with red onion, roasted peppers and a delicious yoghurt hot sauce drizzled over the top, this recipe is glorious. Add some chorizo if you want a non-veggie dinner.

Ingredients

Low calorie cooking spray

50g reduced fat halloumi

¼ tsp smoked paprika

1 small red onion, sliced

100g roasted red pepper, chopped

15g runny honey

5g hot sauce

1 Greek flatbread

60g rocket

Yoghurt drizzle

30g fat-free Greek yoghurt

1 tsp hot sauce

Pinch of salt

Method

- Spray a frying pan with low calorie cooking spray and place over a medium heat. Once hot, add the halloumi to the pan, season with the paprika and fry for 2 minutes. Then add the red onion and roasted red pepper.
- While this cooks, make the yoghurt drizzle by stirring together all the ingredients in a bowl. Set to one side.
- In a small bowl, mix together the honey and hot sauce until well combined. Once the halloumi is toasted on both sides, remove the halloumi and vegetables from the heat and brush the hot honey over the halloumi. Use any remaining hot honey to drizzle over the red onion and pepper.
- Lightly toast the flatbread. Top with the rocket, the vegetables, half of the yoghurt drizzle and finally the halloumi before finishing with the last of the yoghurt drizzle.

Chopped Cheese Sandwiches

Protein 37.8g | Fat 15.0g | Carbs 38.0g

MAKES 2
TAKES 15 minutes

For those who haven't tried these before, they are basically a deconstructed burger in a soft roll. The chopped part comes from the burger patties being broken down into large chunks before adding cheese to fold in for an oozy bite of flavour.

Ingredients

200g lean beef mince
½ tsp garlic granules
½ tsp onion granules
½ tsp smoked paprika
Low calorie cooking spray
1 small white onion, diced
2 cheese singles
2 long white soft rolls (hotdog rolls will work)
10g light butter
20g lighter than light mayonnaise
10g reduced sugar tomato ketchup
1 salad tomato, sliced
2 handfuls of shredded lettuce
Salt and pepper

Method

- In a bowl, season the beef mince with the garlic granules, onion granules, paprika and some salt and pepper. Roll into 2 balls.
- Spray a frying pan with low calorie cooking spray, add the onion and cook over a medium heat for 3 minutes until softened. Push to one side of the pan.
- Add the beef balls and flatten with a spatula. Cook for a few minutes on the first side to get a nice sear. Flip and cook for a further 2 minutes.
- Then you want to start chopping the beef balls into smaller pieces using a spatula. The aim here is to get small chunks of beef but be careful not to break it up too much. Do this quickly to prevent the beef from drying out.
- Fold in the onion before topping with the cheese slices. Leave for 30 seconds before mixing again to ensure the cheese has melted into the beef. Remove from the heat.
- Toast the bread in a pan with the butter for a couple of minutes until golden.
- Spread the bottom of each bun with the mayonnaise and tomato ketchup, then top with the sliced tomato, lettuce and the beef mix.
- To keep the sandwich together, you can wrap it in foil.

Grilled Chicken Stuffed Pitta

Protein 40.0g | Fat 4.9g | Carbs 39.0g

MAKES 2

TAKES 20 minutes, plus 1 hour+ marinating

If you ever want to stray and get a takeaway, put that menu down and reach for these stuffed pittas featuring marinated tender chicken bites and a delicious garlic lemon yoghurt sauce, piled high with shredded lettuce and red onion. Feel free to add any extra salad, such as tomatoes and cucumber, and even pop in a few fries if they fit!

Ingredients

200g chicken breast, diced

1 tbsp fat-free Greek yoghurt

1 tsp smoked paprika

1 tsp tandoori seasoning

1 tsp ground cumin

1 tsp garlic purée

1 tbsp tomato purée

1 tbsp lemon juice

2 pitta breads

50g lettuce, shredded

1 small red onion, sliced

Salt and pepper

Yoghurt sauce

60g fat-free Greek yoghurt

1 tsp chopped garlic

¼ tsp sea salt

1 sprig of fresh coriander, chopped

1 tsp lemon juice

Method

- Mix the chicken in a bowl with the yoghurt, smoked paprika, tandoori seasoning, cumin, garlic purée, tomato purée, lemon juice and salt and pepper. Cover and marinate in the fridge for at least 1 hour.
- Preheat the grill to medium. Add the chicken pieces to a grill rack and grill for 10–12 minutes until the chicken has cooked. Turn partway through cooking . Alternatively, you can cook the chicken in an oven preheated to 190°C/170°C fan for 16 minutes.
- While the chicken is cooking, mix together all the ingredients for the yoghurt sauce and set to one side.
- Toast the pitta breads and slice carefully. Drizzle half of the yoghurt sauce inside each one, add the lettuce, cooked chicken, more yoghurt sauce and the sliced red onion.
- **Air fryer** – Cook the marinated chicken at 185°C for 12 minutes.

Honey Chipotle Chicken and Halloumi Rice

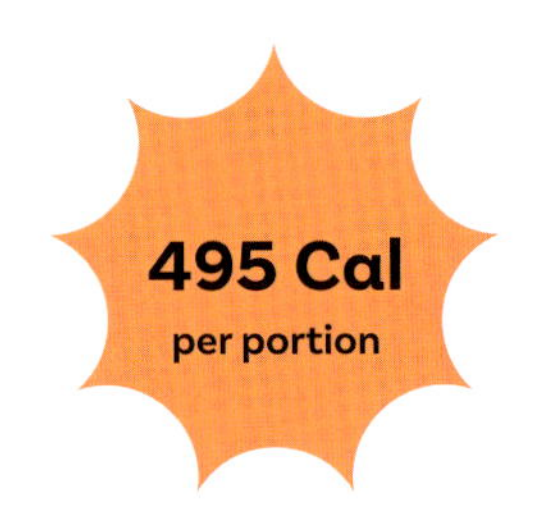

Protein 41.1g | **Fat 17.2g** | **Carbs 41.6g**

SERVES 2
TAKES 20 minutes

I love to cook with chipotle paste. It is such an incredible flavour that pairs divinely with honey and halloumi. This recipe is also perfect for meal prep if you want to make it ahead of time.

Ingredients

Low calorie cooking spray
200g chicken breast, diced
1 tsp smoked paprika
1 tsp dried oregano
1 tsp garlic purée
60g reduced fat halloumi
1 courgette, diced
1 small red pepper, diced
1 small red onion, diced
1 tsp chipotle paste
15g honey
1 tbsp tomato salsa
250g packet of microwave Mexican-style rice
40g peri peri mayonnaise (I use Nando's Perinaise)
3-4 sprigs of fresh parsley, chopped
Salt and pepper

Method

- Set a saucepan over a medium heat and spray with low calorie cooking spray.
- Season the chicken with the smoked paprika, oregano and some salt and pepper to taste. Rub in thoroughly.
- Add the garlic purée to the frying pan, cook for 1-2 minutes, then add the chicken. Pan-fry for 7 minutes.
- While the chicken is cooking, heat a second frying pan over a medium heat and spray with low calorie cooking spray. Dice the halloumi into chunks and, once the pan is hot, fry for 1-2 minutes on each side until golden.
- When the chicken has started to brown, add the courgette, pepper and onion to the chicken pan. Fry for 5 minutes until the vegetables have slightly softened.
- Add the chipotle paste, honey and salsa to the chicken and vegetable pan. Combine well and loosen with a little water if needed.
- Cook the rice according to the packet instructions and add to the chicken and vegetable pan. Top with the halloumi, peri peri mayonnaise and parsley. Serve.

Cheesy Pesto Veg Tartlets

Protein 17.0g | **Fat 22.0g** | **Carbs 35.0g**

MAKES 2

TAKES 30 minutes

Golden flaky pastry filled with cheesy goodness – these vegetable pesto tartlets are the ultimate summer-evening dinner, best served with a side salad. Add a little bit of chicken or even chorizo if you fancy some added protein.

Ingredients

150g reduced fat puff pastry, cut into 2 rectangles

100g cherry tomatoes, halved

75g roasted red peppers, chopped into small squares

40g reduced fat green pesto

Pinch of salt

3–4 fresh basil leaves

100g reduced fat mozzarella

10g Parmesan, grated

Method

- Preheat the oven to 200°C/180°C fan.
- Place the puff pastry rectangles on a piece of baking paper on top of a baking tray. Push out with your hands slightly to make more room around the edges.
- In a bowl, mix together the cherry tomatoes, roasted red peppers, half of the pesto, the salt and 2 torn basil leaves until well combined.
- Spread the remaining pesto in the centre of each puff pastry rectangle, then top with the vegetable mixture from the bowl. Tear the mozzarella over the vegetable mixture. Finish by scattering over the Parmesan.
- Bake in the centre of the oven for 20 minutes until golden. Finish with the remaining basil leaves.

Buffalo Chicken Rice Bake

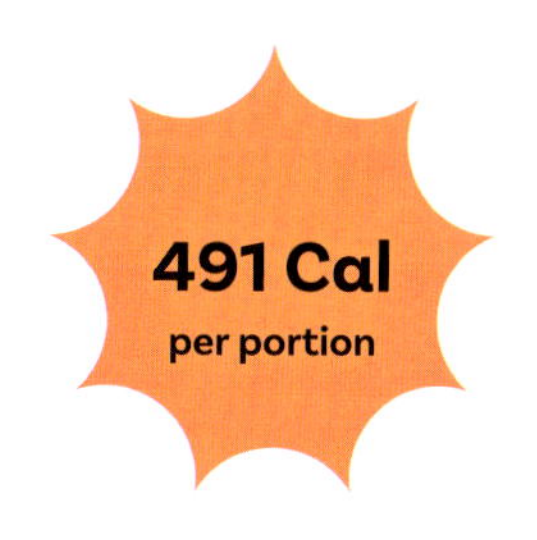

Protein 41.6g | **Fat 9.1g** | **Carbs 57.0g**

SERVES 2
TAKES 30 minutes

Buffalo sauce has not that long come on to my radar and now I can't get enough. Don't be put off if spicy food isn't your jam, it isn't that hot (I suck at eating spicy food). You could use this recipe for meal prep, but if you plan to reheat, add the yoghurt sauce fresh.

Ingredients

125g packet of boil-in-the-bag long-grain rice
200g chicken breast, diced
2 tsp smoked paprika
2 tsp garlic granules
2 tsp onion granules
1 tsp dried chives
Low calorie cooking spray
1 white onion, diced
4 celery sticks, chopped
1 tsp garlic purée
200ml chicken stock
40g buffalo sauce
50g tomato salsa
40g mozzarella, grated
2 spring onions, diced
Salt and pepper

Herby yoghurt sauce

50g fat-free natural yoghurt
½ tsp garlic granules
½ tsp onion granules
¼ tsp dried chives
¼ tsp dried dill
¼ tsp dried parsley

Method

- Cook the bag of rice for 2 minutes less than the packet instructions.
- Season the chicken with 1 teaspoon of the smoked paprika, 1 teaspoon of the garlic granules, 1 teaspoon of the onion granules, the dried chives and salt and pepper to taste.
- Spray a medium frying pan with low calorie cooking spray and heat over a medium heat. Once hot, fry the onion and celery in the garlic purée for 4–5 minutes until softened.
- Add the chicken and fry for 8–10 minutes until almost cooked through. Then add the rice and cook for a further 2 minutes before adding the remaining smoked paprika, garlic granules and onion granules, the chicken stock, 30g of the buffalo sauce and the salsa. Leave to simmer and reduce for 5–8 minutes.
- Top with the cheese and leave over a medium heat for a couple of minutes until the cheese has melted.
- To make the herby yoghurt sauce, mix all the ingredients together in a small bowl.
- Serve, drizzling over the herby yoghurt sauce, the remaining 10g buffalo sauce and the spring onions.

Smashed Cheeseburger Tacos

Protein 40.6g | **Fat 19.0g** | **Carbs 38.8g**

SERVES 2
TAKES 15 minutes

These tacos are such a delicious midweek meal. The flavours from the beef end up coated onto the taco, making them slightly crispy. Piled high with shredded lettuce, onion, gherkins, cheese and homemade burger sauce, be warned that you will be addicted!

Ingredients

200g lean beef mince
1 tsp garlic granules
1 tsp onion granules
Low calorie cooking spray
4 mini tortilla wraps
4 light cheese singles
150g lettuce, shredded
½ small white onion, finely diced
4 baby gherkins, finely diced
Salt and pepper

Sauce

40g lighter than light mayonnaise
15g reduced sugar tomato ketchup
½ tsp yellow mustard
Pinch of salt
4 baby gherkins, chopped
1 tsp white wine vinegar

Method

- In a bowl, season the beef mince with the garlic and onion granules and a pinch of salt and pepper. Roll into 4 equal balls.
- Mix together all the ingredients for the sauce and set to one side.
- Spray a pan with low calorie cooking spray and place over a medium heat. Add a beef ball to the top of each wrap and, using your hands, press the balls and spread carefully to cover the wraps.
- Place a wrap in the pan, beef-side down. Press down on the back with a spatula and leave undisturbed for a few minutes. Use a spatula to carefully flip the wrap over, then place a cheese single over the centre. Leave for 1½ minutes, then remove from the pan. Repeat with the remaining wraps and cheese.
- Top each wrap with lettuce, white onion and gherkins before drizzling over the burger sauce.

Cajun Honey BBQ Chicken Pasta

Protein 47.0g | **Fat 7.5g** | **Carbs 74.7g**

SERVES 2
TAKES 25 minutes

A speedy pasta dish filled with delicious flavours that will have you hooked.

Ingredients

Low calorie cooking spray
200g chicken breast, diced
2 tsp Cajun seasoning
2 tsp smoked paprika
2 tsp dried oregano
130g pasta
1 tsp garlic purée
1 red onion, diced
1 green pepper, diced
25g honey
1 tbsp soy sauce
50g barbecue sauce
220g tinned chopped tomatoes
40g reduced fat mature Cheddar
Salt and pepper

Garnish (optional)

sliced spring onions
dried parsley

Method

- Spray an ovenproof frying pan with low calorie cooking spray and set over a medium heat. Season the chicken with 1 teaspoon each of the Cajun seasoning, smoked paprika and oregano and some salt and pepper (to taste). Pan-fry for 10–12 minutes until almost cooked and remove from the pan.
- Cook the pasta according to the packet instructions. While the pasta cooks, add the garlic purée to the frying pan along with the onion and green pepper. Fry for 4 minutes.
- Add the honey, soy sauce, barbecue sauce and remaining seasonings to the pan, followed by the chopped tomatoes. Shred the cooked chicken and add to the mixture.
- Add the cooked and drained pasta and mix well. Top with the cheese and melt under the grill (or you can also cover the pan with a lid and use the hob).
- Garnish with spring onions and dried parsley to finish, if you like

Tandoori Chicken Naan Melt

Protein 47.0g | Fat 8.9g | Carbs 51.2g

MAKES 1
TAKES 20 minutes

Who knew that naans would be perfect for a toastie-style recipe? This melt is packed full of a quick tandoori chicken, cheese, peppers and onions, which is then sandwiched between two mini naans for a mouthwatering bite every single time.

Ingredients

100g chicken breast
¼ tsp ginger purée
¼ tsp garlic purée
1 tsp lemon juice
20g tandoori paste (I use Patak's)
30g fat-free natural yoghurt
Low calorie cooking spray
½ small red onion, diced
30g sliced frozen peppers (I buy the pre-sliced kind)
2 mini naans
15g reduced fat Cheddar (or Eatlean cheese), grated
5g mozzarella, grated
Salt and pepper
Mango chutney, to serve (optional)

Method

- Begin by mixing the chicken with the ginger and garlic purées, lemon juice and tandoori paste. Add 20g of the yoghurt, stir to combine, then cover with clingfilm and refrigerate for as long as possible (even 5 minutes is better than nothing).
- Once ready to use, spray a frying pan with low calorie cooking spray and set over a medium heat. Add the chicken and red onion and cook for 10 minutes. Remove the chicken from the pan and, on a chopping board, shred the chicken into smaller pieces. Return to the pan and add the peppers.
- When the chicken is fully cooked, remove from the heat and stir through the remaining yoghurt.
- Add the chicken to one of the mini naans, top with both the grated cheeses and the remaining naan.
- Pan-fry in a clean frying pan for 3–4 minutes on each side until golden and the cheese has melted.
- Serve with a dunk in some mango chutney (optional but highly recommended!).

If you have a panini press, use this for step 5. You can also place another pan on top to help flatten the sandwich further.

Tex Mex Sweet Potato and Black Bean Rice

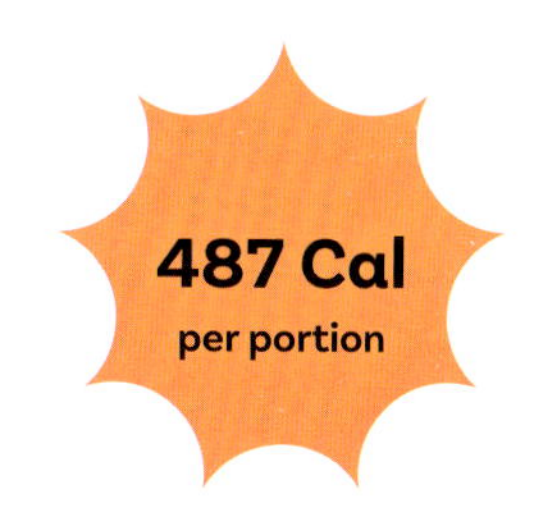

Protein 20.3g | Fat 6.3g | Carbs 84.6g

SERVES 2

TAKES 25 minutes

Mexican-inspired flavours work really well with black beans and sweet potato for a veggie-friendly dinner. If you fancy some meat with this recipe, reduce the rice and add some lean beef mince or diced chorizo. This meal is already speedy but if you're in a super dash, use Mexican-flavoured microwave rice.

Ingredients

90g quick-cook long-grain white rice

150g sweet potato

Low calorie cooking spray

1 tsp garlic purée

1 white onion, diced

2 tsp ground cumin

½ tsp mild chilli powder

2 tsp smoked paprika

1 tsp dried oregano

150g tinned black beans, drained

1 tsp chipotle paste

1 tbsp lime juice

60g tomato salsa

100ml water

40g reduced fat Cheddar, grated

Handful of fresh coriander, chopped

Salt and pepper

Method

- Cook the rice according to the packet instructions.
- While the rice is cooking, peel and dice the sweet potato into cubes. Place in a microwavable dish, cover and heat on high for 2 minutes. Leave with the lid on to allow the sweet potato to continue cooking.
- Spray a pan with low calorie cooking spray, add the garlic purée and onion and cook over a medium heat for 3–4 minutes until slightly softened.
- Once the onion has softened, add the sweet potato, 1 teaspoon of the cumin, the chilli powder, 1 teaspoon of the smoked paprika, the oregano and salt and pepper to taste. Mix well and fry for 2 minutes, then add the black beans, chipotle paste and lime juice.
- Continue to cook over a medium-low heat while the rice is cooking. When the rice is ready, drain and add to the sweet potato pan, along with the salsa, remaining cumin and smoked paprika and the water.
- Stir, then top with the cheese. Cover with a lid for a couple of minutes until the cheese has melted.
- Garnish with the fresh coriander to serve.

Four

DINE IN AT HOME

Garlic Butter Steak Bites

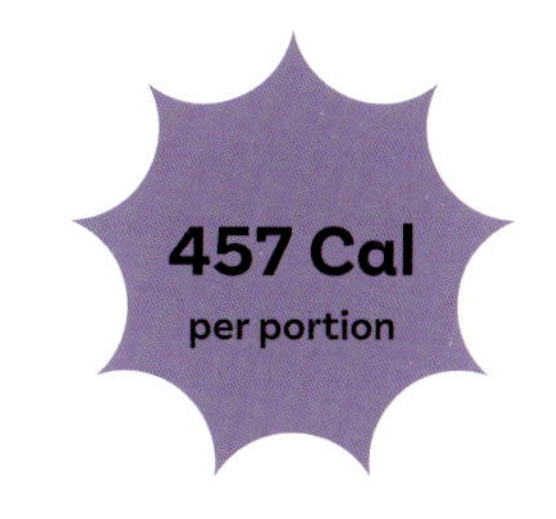

Protein 31.5g | **Fat 17.0g** | **Carbs 42.0g**

SERVES 2
TAKES 30 minutes

The steak in this recipe is so juicy. It's seared for ultimate flavour before being tossed in the most addictive garlic butter sauce. This recipe is best served with mashed potato and green vegetables for the ultimate dining experience at home.

Ingredients

200g sirloin steak, fat removed and diced

1 tsp garlic powder

Olive oil spray

20g light butter

1 tsp garlic purée

1 shallot, finely diced

1 tsp dried thyme

1 tbsp Worcestershire sauce

Salt and pepper

Mashed potato

450g golden potatoes, peeled and quartered

1 tsp garlic powder

1 sprig of fresh thyme, leaves picked

30g light cream cheese, at room temperature

1 tbsp reduced fat soured cream

30ml skimmed milk, at room temperature

Method

- Cook the potatoes in a large pan of boiling salted water for 15–20 minutes until almost tender.
- Season the steak with the garlic powder and some salt and pepper. Give a few sprays of olive oil before rubbing the seasoning in thoroughly.
- When the potatoes are almost tender, heat a frying pan over a medium-high heat. Spray the pan with a couple of squirts of olive oil.
- Once the oil is hot, add the steak. Leave undisturbed for a minute, then flip for a further minute and remove the steak from the pan.
- Drain the potatoes, then add the garlic powder, season with salt and pepper to taste and add the thyme, cream cheese, soured cream and milk. Mash well until smooth.
- Reduce the heat under the frying pan, then add the butter, garlic purée and shallot. Cook for a minute before adding salt, pepper, the thyme and Worcestershire sauce.
- Return the steak to the pan for a minute, tossing in the sauce.
- Serve the steak bites immediately over the creamy mashed potato.

Marry Me Linguine

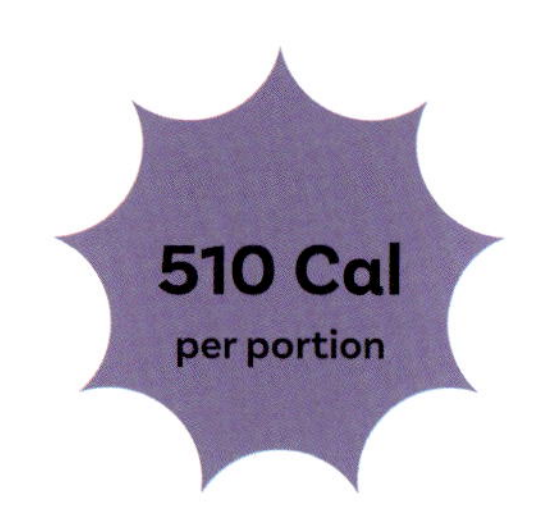

Protein 40.6g | **Fat 13.0g** | **Carbs 54.8g**

SERVES 2
TAKES 30 minutes

Be warned – this recipe will cause love. Even if you aren't dropping on one knee for someone else, the creamy sauce will have you falling in love with yourself. Linguine helps to mop up all of the incredible sauce for the optimum bite.

Ingredients

Low calorie cooking spray
200g chicken breast
1 tsp onion powder
1 tsp garlic powder
2 tsp smoked paprika
2 tsp dried oregano
120g dried linguine
1 small white onion, diced
1 tsp garlic purée
1 tsp tomato purée
100ml chicken stock
40g sun-dried tomatoes, roughly chopped
100ml reduced fat single cream
10g Parmesan
A few sprigs of fresh parsley, chopped
Salt and pepper

Method

- Heat a large frying pan over a medium heat and spray with low calorie cooking spray. Season the chicken with the onion powder, garlic powder, 1 teaspoon of the smoked paprika, 1 teaspoon of the oregano and salt and pepper to taste. Pan-fry the chicken for 4 minutes on each side until there is a nice sear. Remove from the pan.
- Cook the pasta according to the packet instructions. Drain, retaining a good cup of the pasta cooking water.
- In the same frying pan, start on the sauce. Fry the onion over a medium heat for 2–3 minutes until slightly softened, then add the garlic purée, tomato purée, chicken stock, sun-dried tomatoes, cream and the remaining smoked paprika and oregano. Mix well and return the chicken to the pan for 10 minutes until the sauce has reduced.
- Once the sauce has reduced, remove the chicken, stir through the Parmesan and loosen with the reserved pasta water (I used 80ml).
- Slice the chicken and use it to top the pasta along with any leftover sauce and the chopped parsley.

Katsu Fish Finger Sandwich

Protein 35.3g | **Fat 8.9g** | **Carbs 59.4g**

MAKES 2
TAKES 25 minutes

AF

Fish paired with curry sauce is a banging combo. Layer that upon a crusty roll with zingy lemon mayonnaise and you have a boujee sandwich you will want on repeat! Most white fish would work here, so use what you like and if you are really anti fish, sub for chicken instead.

Ingredients

1 tsp olive oil
1 tbsp mild curry powder
1 tsp cornflour
2 tbsp light soy sauce
½ tsp ginger purée
½ tsp garlic purée
120ml chicken stock
250g skinless, boneless basa fillets
Low calorie cooking spray
35g panko breadcrumbs
2 white crusty rolls
30g lighter than light mayonnaise
1 tsp lemon juice
½ tsp dried coriander
½ little gem lettuce, chopped
¼ small red onion, finely diced

Method

- Add the olive oil, ½ tablespoon of the curry powder and the cornflour to a saucepan and mix together over a medium heat. Add 1 tablespoon of the light soy sauce, ¼ teaspoon of the ginger purée, ¼ teaspoon of the garlic purée and the chicken stock. Whisk together until there are no lumps and leave over a very low heat. If it thickens too much near the time of serving, add a tablespoon of water to loosen.
- Pat the basa fillets dry with kitchen paper, then slice into strips. Trasnfer to a bowl, add the remaining ¼ teaspoon of ginger purée, ¼ teaspoon of garlic purée and 1 tablespoon of light soy sauce. Mix well to coat.
- Spray a baking tray with low calorie cooking spray and preheat the oven to 200°C/180°C fan.
- On a plate, mix together the breadcrumbs and the remaining ½ tablespoon of curry powder. Dip each fish strip into the breadcrumb mixture, pressing the crumbs in well to adhere.
- Place the strips on the baking tray, spray with low calorie cooking spray and bake in the oven for 15 minutes, turning partway through.
- Slice the rolls and place them in the oven for a few minutes to ensure that they are well toasted.
- Meanwhile, mix together the mayonnaise, lemon juice and coriander.
- Grab the buns, spread with the mayonnaise, add the lettuce and stack the fish fingers on top of each other, then drizzle over the katsu sauce and finish with the red onion.
- **Air fryer** – Cook the coated fish fingers at 185°C for 10–12 minutes.

Baked Creamy Garlic Herb Orzo

Protein 12.5g | Fat 16.0g | Carbs 48.0g

SERVES 4
TAKES 30 minutes

This dish deserves a medal for how tasty it is. Partially cooking the orzo cuts down a huge amount of time usually spent waiting for the stock to thicken. For an added protein boost, chicken should be your go-to, and for extra veggies courgette or mushrooms are delicious too. If orzo isn't your jam, other pastas do work with this recipe!

Ingredients

150g block of garlic herb cheese

250g cherry tomatoes

Olive oil spray

240g dried orzo

1 tsp garlic granules

1 tsp smoked paprika

½ tsp dried oregano

400ml vegetable stock

½ tsp chipotle paste

100g baby spinach

Salt and pepper

Method

- Preheat the oven to 180°C/160°C fan.
- To a large baking dish, add the garlic herb cheese and cherry tomatoes, spray with olive oil and bake in the oven for 10 minutes.
- Add the orzo to a pan of boiling salted water and parboil (cook for half the time stated on the packet). Drain the orzo fully and add it to the baking dish.
- Season the orzo with the garlic granules, smoked paprika and oregano and season with salt and pepper. Toss the orzo with the tomatoes to combine.
- Mix together the vegetable stock and chipotle paste, then pour over the dish. Return to the oven for 5 minutes.
- Remove from the oven, stir in the spinach, then return to the oven for a few more minutes until the spinach has wilted.
- Once the spinach has wilted, break up the garlic herb cheese, swirling around the dish to make it creamy.

Sticky Halloumi Noodles

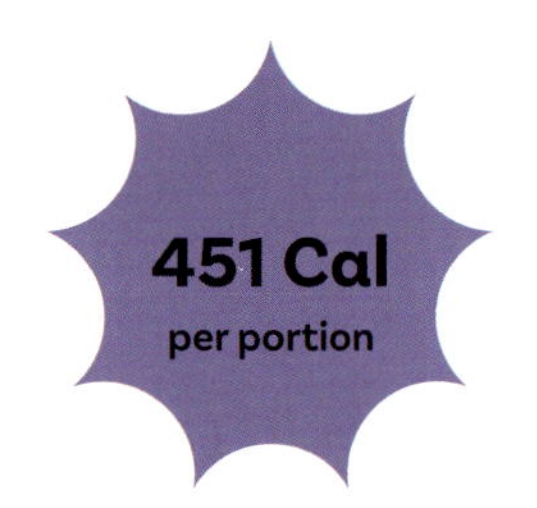

Protein 24.7g | Fat 12.0g | Carbs 71.0g

SERVES 2

TAKES 20 minutes

Do you ever have the urge to eat straight out of the pan? Well, this is the recipe where you will want to do just that! Sticky, sweet and salty, this halloumi is banging with noodles and the ultimate meat-free dish.

Ingredients

2 nests of egg noodles

Low calorie cooking spray

120g reduced fat halloumi, sliced

1 tsp garlic purée

1 red pepper, cut into strips

4 pak choi leaves, chopped

3 spring onions, chopped and green and white parts separated

Sauce

3 tbsp reduced sugar sweet chilli sauce

2 tbsp light soy sauce

1 tbsp dark soy sauce

20g runny honey

1 tbsp reduced sugar tomato ketchup

1 tbsp water

Method

- Add the nests of noodles to a pan of boiling water and cook according to the packet instructions. Drain and rinse with cold water to prevent sticking.
- Spray a frying pan with low calorie cooking spray, then add the sliced halloumi and cook over a medium heat for 4–5 minutes, turning occasionally, until golden.
- Mix together all of the ingredients for the sauce.
- Add half the sauce to the pan and cook for a minute, then add the garlic purée, red pepper, pak choi and the white parts of the spring onions. Fry for a couple of minutes, then add the noodles and remaining sauce. Combine well.
- Serve immediately, scattered with the green parts of the spring onions.

Pulled Chipotle Beef Chilli

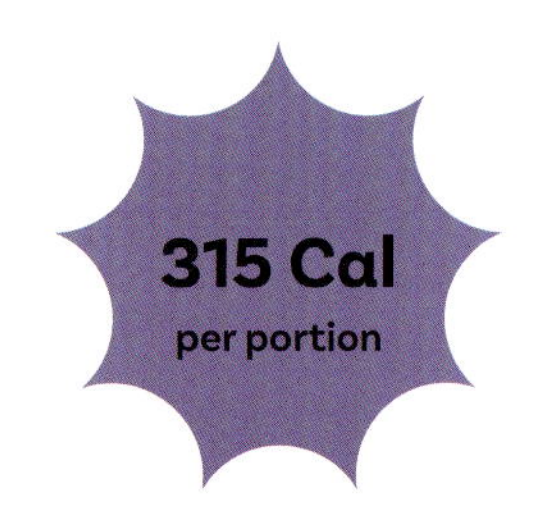

Protein 49.0g | Fat 7.6g | Carbs 34.2g

SERVES 3
TAKES 3 hours

A delicious pulled chilli beef made with chipotle for added depth of flavour. I like to serve this over fluffy white rice, with reduced fat sour cream, some fresh coriander and chilli tortilla chips, but it is also just as tasty with potatoes or pasta.

Ingredients

400g lean diced beef
1 white onion, diced
1 red pepper, diced
1 tbsp ground cumin
1 tsp mixed herbs
1 tsp smoked paprika
1 tsp ground coriander
2 beef stock cubes, crumbled
1 tsp chipotle paste
1 heaped tsp garlic purée
1 tbsp tomato purée
1 tsp coffee granules (optional)
400g tin of chopped tomatoes
100ml water
1 tsp granulated sweetener (optional)

Method

- Preheat the oven to 140°C/120°C fan.
- Start by browning the beef in a hot frying pan for 4–5 minutes until there is a nice sear all over. This is optional but recommended.
- Add the beef, onion, pepper, cumin, mixed herbs, smoked paprika, coriander and crumbled stock cubes to a large casserole dish and give it all a good stir.
- Then add the chipotle paste, garlic purée, tomato purée, coffee granules (if using), chopped tomatoes, water and sweetener, if using. Stir until well combined.
- Cover and cook in the oven for 2½ hours. Stir the chilli partway through if needed, and add another 100ml of water if it starts to dry up.
- Once the cooking time is up, pull the beef apart using 2 forks, or use the back of a wooden spoon and push it down so it falls apart.
- **Slow cooker** – Sear the beef as in step 2, then transfer to the slow cooker with all the remaining ingredients. Give everything a good stir and cook on low for 7 hours or high for 5 hours. If cooking for less time, omit the water and judge near the end of the cooking time if you need to loosen the sauce.

Crispy Chicken and Feta Pasta

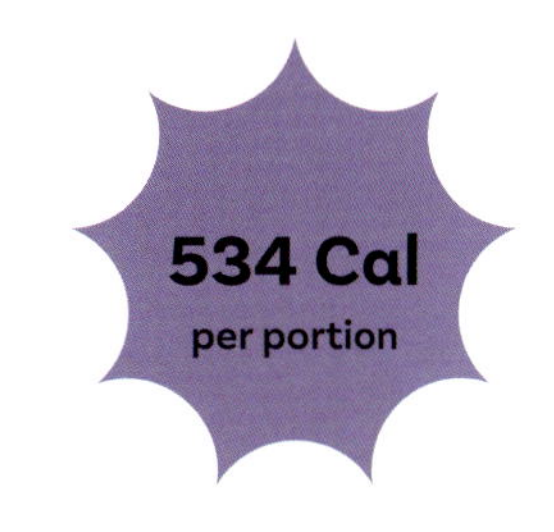

Protein 43.8g | Fat 8.2g | Carbs 67.0g

SERVES 2
TAKES 35 minutes

Bold and vibrant, this crispy panko chicken served with a creamy feta pepper sauce looks and tastes deluxe. Pair with a rocket salad for a showstopping dinner that you deserve.

Ingredients

Low calorie cooking spray
1 white onion, chopped
1 red pepper, sliced
1 tsp garlic purée
200g tinned chopped tomatoes
1 tsp Cajun seasoning
2 tsp smoked paprika
2 tsp dried oregano
200g chicken breasts
1 egg, beaten
30g panko breadcrumbs
120g dried pasta (any shape will do)
50g feta
1 tsp lemon juice
A few sprigs of fresh parsley, chopped
Chilli flakes, to taste
Salt and pepper

Method

- Spray a frying pan with low calorie cooking spray and set over a medium heat. Fry the onion, red pepper and garlic purée for a few minutes. Add the chopped tomatoes along with some salt and pepper (to taste), the Cajun seasoning, and half the smoked paprika and oregano. Leave to simmer while you prepare the chicken.
- Preheat the oven to 185°C/165°C fan.
- Flatten the chicken breasts by wrapping them loosely in clingfilm and squashing with a rolling pin. Unwrap and season with the remaining smoked paprika and oregano. Using tongs or forks, dip each breast in the egg, shaking off any excess, and then dip in the panko breadcrumbs. Spray lightly with low calorie cooking spray and place on a baking tray. Bake in the oven for 20 minutes.
- While the chicken is in the oven, cook the pasta according to the packet instructions, drain and set aside.
- Transfer the chopped tomato mixture to a blender along with 40g of the feta cheese.
- Return to the pan, add the lemon juice, half of the parsley and chilli flakes (to your desired heat level) and simmer for 15 minutes.
- Once the chicken is cooked, slice into strips. Stir three-quarters of the sauce through the pasta. Top with the sliced chicken and pour over the remaining sauce.
- Finish with the reamining parsley, some chilli flakes and the remaining 10g feta crumbled over the top.

Crispy Bang Bang Salmon Bites

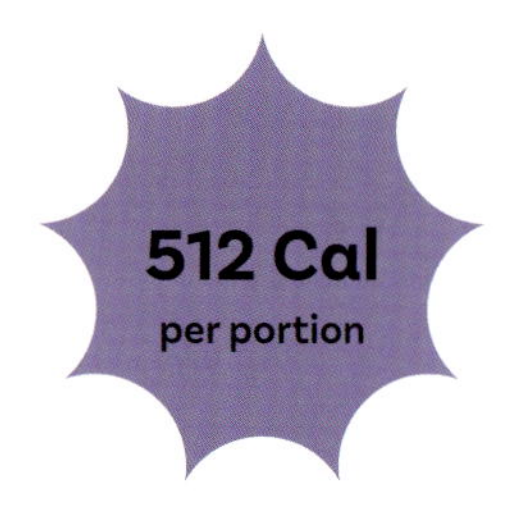

Protein 30.7g | Fat 15.1g | Carbs 62.9g

SERVES 2

TAKES 25 minutes

I have to say, bang bang sauce is next level with crispy bites of salmon. Bang bang sauce is a mixture of mayo, sweet chilli sauce and sriracha that is seriously addictive. I like to have some Tenderstem broccoli with this recipe for the perfect dining experience. If you don't like fish, use chicken instead.

Ingredients

2 salmon fillets

1 tsp garlic powder

1 tsp smoked paprika

Low calorie cooking spray

40g panko breadcrumbs

250g packet of microwave sticky rice

1 tbsp black sesame seeds

2 spring onions, diced

Salt

Bang bang sauce

15g reduced sugar sweet chilli sauce

15g sriracha sauce

70g lighter than light mayonnaise

Method

- Preheat the oven to 180°C/160°C fan.
- Combine all the sauce ingredients in a bowl and set to one side. Add water if needed to make a thinner consistency (about 3 tablespoons).
- Dice the salmon into chunks and remove the skin.
- In a shallow bowl, season the salmon with the garlic powder, smoked paprika and some salt to taste. Pour half of the bang bang sauce into the bowl and stir to coat the salmon.
- Spray a baking tray with low calorie cooking spray. Dip each salmon chunk into the panko breadcrumbs and transfer to the baking tray in a single layer.
- Bake in the oven for 15 minutes.
- When the salmon is nearly ready, cook the rice according to the packet instructions.
- Dvide the rice between 2 bowls, top with the crispy salmon bites, drizzle over the remaining sauce and top with the sesame seeds and spring onions.

Chicken Alfredo

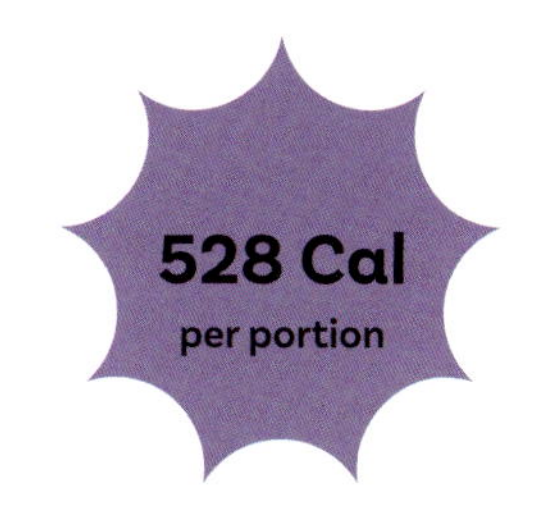

Protein 43.1g | **Fat 16.0g** | **Carbs 54.7g**

SERVES 2
TAKES 30 minutes

Pasta drenched in a rich and creamy sauce paired with seasoned juicy chicken – I am drooling as I'm thinking about it right now. Good as an occasional treat, but after you see how easy it is to make, it'll be on your menu more often than not.

Ingredients

2 chicken breasts (around 100g each)
1 tsp garlic granules
1 tsp onion granules
1 tsp smoked paprika
120g dried linguine
15g light butter
1 tsp garlic purée
150ml chicken stock
100ml reduced fat single cream
1 tsp Italian herb seasoning
20g Parmesan, grated
30g lightest cream cheese, at room temperature
3 sprigs of fresh parsley, finely chopped
Salt and pepper

Method

- Preheat the oven to 180°C/160°C fan.
- Season the chicken breasts with the garlic granules, onion granules and smoked paprika. Rub the spices in thoroughly, then place on a baking tray or in an ovenproof dish and bake in the oven for 18 minutes.
- While the chicken cooks, add the pasta to a pan of boiling salted water and cook until al dente.
- Add the butter and garlic purée to a saucepan and let it melt over a low heat before mixing together. Add the chicken stock, cream and Italian herb seasoning along with a pinch of salt and pepper and turn up to a medium-high heat.
- Once the sauce has reduced by half, add the Parmesan, cream cheese and half of the parsley, mix well and turn the heat back down to a simmer.
- Once cooked, combine most of the creamy sauce with the pasta. Serve alongside the chicken, drizzling over the remaining sauce and sprinkling with the remaining chopped parsley.

Creamy Peri Peri Steak and Potatoes with Lemon Garlic Broccoli

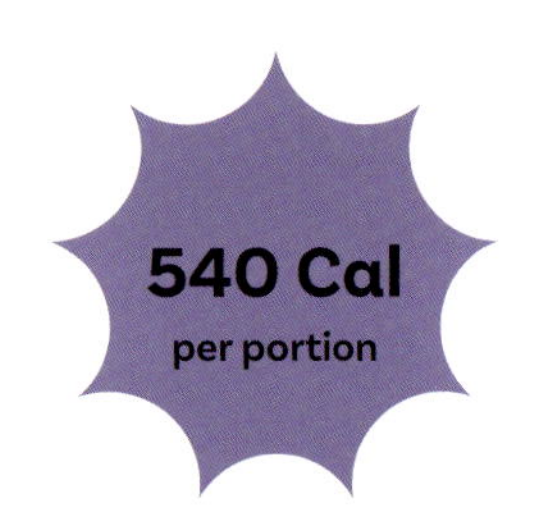

Protein 36.6g | Fat 18.0g | Carbs 56.0g

SERVES 2
TAKES 35 minutes

This recipe really does give restaurant vibes but in the comfort of your own home. The creamy peri peri sauce pops this dish off – you'll be left wanting more and more.

Ingredients

400g Maris Piper potatoes
4 tsp garlic peri peri rub
200g thin-cut sirloin steaks
3 tsp lemon juice
2 tsp garlic purée
80ml chicken stock
1 tsp tomato purée
100ml reduced fat single cream
1 tbsp peri peri sauce
20g Parmesan, grated
Handful of chopped fresh parsley
100g Tenderstem broccoli

Method

- Preheat the oven to 180°C/160°C fan.
- Cut the potatoes into small cubes. Pat dry with kitchen paper, then season with salt, pepper and 1 teaspoon of the peri peri rub. Bake in the oven for 35 minutes, shaking throughout.
- While the potatoes are cooking, rub the steak with 1 teaspoon of the peri peri rub and 1 teaspoon of the lemon juice. Leave to marinate while you work on the sauce.
- Add 1 teaspoon of.the garlic purée and the remaining 1 teaspoon of peri peri rub to a saucepan, along with the stock and tomato purée. Mix well, then add the cream and peri peri sauce. Bring to a simmer over a medium heat and leave for 10 minutes, then stir through the Parmesan and parsley.
- Next, cook the broccoli in salted water for 3–4 minutes until tender.
- While the broccoli cooks, pan-fry the steak in a frying pan over a high heat. For medium-rare, cook for 1–1½ minutes on each side, depending on the thickness of the steak. Remove from the pan, leave to rest and then slice.
- Once the broccoli is done, in the same steak pan, add the remaining teaspoon of garlic purée and 2 teaspoons of lemon juice. Fry for a minute.
- Serve the potatoes, steak and broccoli with the sauce drizzled over.
- **Air fryer** – Cook the seasoned potatoes at 185°C for 25 minutes, shaking throughout.

French Dip Baguettes

Protein 36.9g | Fat 15.0g | Carbs 44.9g

SERVES 2
TAKES 20 minutes

I love a French dip as much as the next person but what I can't be bothered with is slow roasting beef when I want a quick meal. With a few shortcuts this recipe replicates that delicious, tender, mouthwatering sandwich with a tasty jus for extra dunking.

Ingredients

200g rib-eye steak
1 tsp garlic granules
1 tsp onion granules
1 tsp dried oregano
2 bake-at-home baguettes (I use Tesco bake at home)
1 small white onion, sliced
1 tsp garlic purée
1 tsp dried thyme
1 tbsp Worcestershire sauce
1 tbsp light soy sauce
150ml beef stock
40g mozzarella, grated
Salt and pepper

Method

- Preheat the oven to 180°C/160°C fan.
- Season the steak with the garlic granules, onion granules, oregano, and some salt and pepper. In a large frying pan over a high heat, pan-fry each steak for 1½ minutes on each side. Set aside to rest.
- Bake the baguettes according to the packet instructions.
- While the bread bakes, add the onion to the steak pan, along with the garlic purée, thyme, Worcestershire sauce, soy sauce and beef stock. Bring to the boil and simmer for 10 minutes until it has thickened. This is your jus.
- Once cooked, halve the baguettes lengthways. Turn down the heat to 140°C/120°C fan. Thinly slice the steak and add the slices to the baguettes along with the cheese. Pop back in the oven for a minute until the cheese is melted.
- Pour the jus into serving dishes to dunk the sandwiches in.

Creamy Chicken and Broccoli Pie

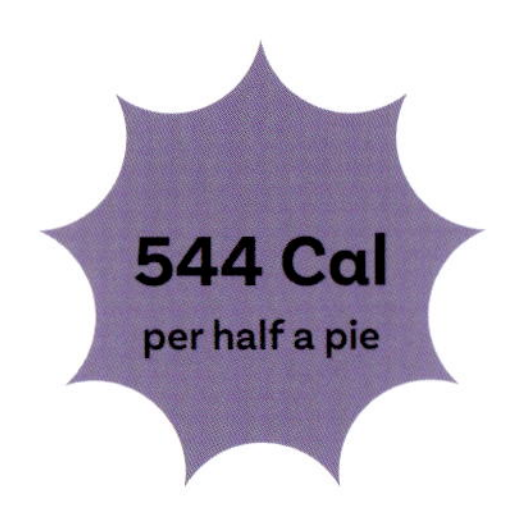

Protein 43.3g | **Fat 17.0g** | **Carbs 40.9g**

SERVES 2
TAKES 45 minutes

This recipe is so easy to make, it almost feels criminal that it tastes so good. I always used to be put off by pies because of the high calorie count, but that is where light puff pastry comes in to give us a hand. I like to serve this with some seasonal veggies.

Ingredients

200g chicken breast

1 tsp garlic granules

1 tsp onion granules

150g broccoli, chopped into small pieces

400ml tin of chicken soup

50ml chicken stock

40g sage and onion stuffing made up according to packet instructions

150g light ready-rolled puff pastry sheet

1 egg, beaten

Method

- Preheat the oven to 180°C/160°C fan.
- Season the chicken with the garlic and onion granules. Rub in thoroughly and place in an 18 x 30cm ovenproof dish. Bake in the oven for 18 minutes. Once cooked, chop the chicken into small chunks. Don't turn your oven off.
- Transfer the chicken to a baking dish along with the broccoli. Pour over the chicken soup along with the chicken stock. Combine well before topping with the stuffing.
- Cut your pastry to the size of your dish and spread it over the dish to cover the pie filling. Pop in some air holes using a fork if you want it less puffy!
- Brush some beaten egg over the pastry, then bake in the oven for 25 minutes.

Garlic Herb Parmesan Steak Sandwich

Protein 36.5g | **Fat 16.0g** | **Carbs 43.7g**

SERVES 2
TAKES 20 minutes

Nothing beats a steak sandwich for a boujee dinner at home. Pair that with a delicious homemade sauce and every bite will have you eye rolling at how delicious it tastes. I like to serve these sandwiches with a few smashed baby potatoes and salad.

Ingredients

Low calorie cooking spray
1 white onion, sliced
1 tsp garlic purée
1 tbsp Worcestershire sauce
200g steak (I use rib-eye)
2 part-baked rolls
15g 50% less fat garlic and herb cream cheese
Handful of rocket
Salt and pepper

Sauce

150ml beef stock
½ tsp smoked paprika
½ tsp garlic powder
½ tsp onion powder
½ tsp dried thyme
½ dried tsp rosemary
35g 50% less fat garlic and herb cream cheese
20g Parmesan, grated

Method

- Start by spraying a large frying pan with low calorie cooking spray and placing it over a medium heat. Fry the onion in the garlic purée and Worcestershire sauce. Add a tablespoon of water and cook for 5–7 minutes until they become brown and softened. Turn down the heat to low.
- Rub the steak with salt and pepper and set to one side.
- Add the beef stock to a saucepan along with all the seasonings for the sauce. Heat over a medium heat for a couple of minutes before stirring through the cream cheese. Turn up the heat to medium for 5 minutes. Add the Parmesan and leave over a medium heat, stirring occasionally.
- Bake the rolls according to the packet instructions.
- While the rolls cook, heat a large frying pan and cook the steak, depending on its thickness, for 1½ minutes on each side. Leave to rest for 5 minutes before slicing into strips.
- Spread half of the cream cheese on each bread roll, top with the steak, onions, the creamy sauce and some rocket. Use any remaining sauce for dipping.

Baked Broccoli Gnocchi

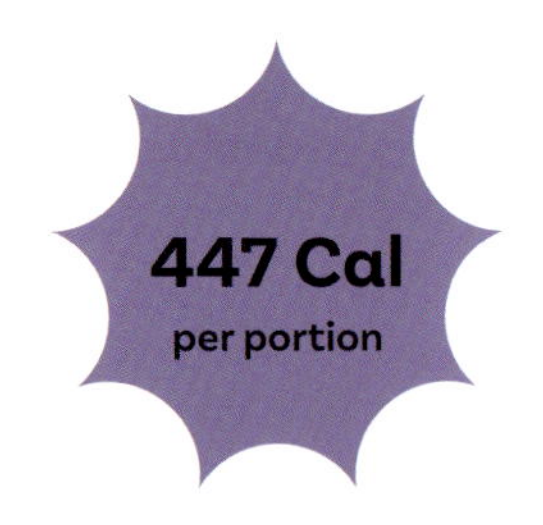

Protein 19.7g | Fat 12.9g | Carbs 60.4g

SERVES 2
TAKES 25 minutes

Broccoli and creamy cheesy sauces go hand in hand, then pair that with pillowy bites of gnocchi and you've got a drool-worthy dinner. Lean diced bacon baked on top is a perfect choice for those who wish to add some meat.

Ingredients

200g broccoli, cut into small florets
Low calorie cooking spray
400g dried gnocchi
60g reduced fat soft cream cheese
150ml chicken stock
1 tsp garlic granules
1 tsp onion granules
1 tsp mustard
2 tbsp reduced fat crème fraîche
45g mozzarella, grated
5g Parmesan, grated
Salt and pepper

Method

- Preheat the oven to 170°C/150°C fan.
- In a large saucepan filled with salted water, bring the broccoli to the boil for 5 minutes until slightly softened, then drain.
- Meanwhile, spray a medium frying pan with low calorie cooking spray. Add the gnocchi and pan-fry for a couple of minutes until slightly toasted.
- Remove from the pan and set to one side.
- In the same pan, put the cream cheese, chicken stock, garlic granules, onion granules, mustard and salt and pepper to taste. Combine well until thickened over a medium heat.
- Transfer to a baking dish, add the gnocchi and broccoli and stir through the crème fraîche before topping with the grated cheeses. Bake in the oven for 10 minutes.

Creamy Lemon Garlic Chicken

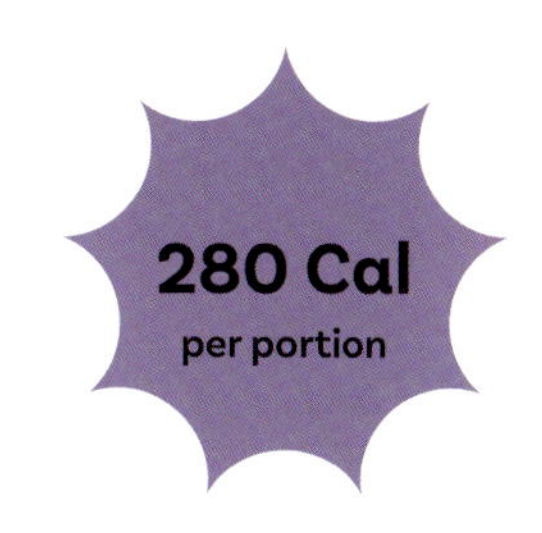

Protein 33.6g | **Fat 12.9g** | **Carbs 7.2g**

SERVES 2
TAKES 30 minutes

Smoky chicken pieces drizzled in a creamy garlic lemon Parmesan sauce for a boujee dinner at home. Serve over mashed potato or long-grain rice with Tenderstem broccoli for a flavoursome dinner.

Ingredients

200g chicken breast, diced

1½ tsp smoked paprika

1 tsp onion granules

1 tsp garlic granules

1 tsp dried parsley

Squeeze of lemon juice

Low calorie cooking spray

5g light butter

1½ tsp garlic purée

100ml 45% less fat single cream

20g Parmesan, grated

A few sprigs of fresh parsley, chopped

2 spring onions, diced

Chilli flakes

Salt and pepper

Method

- In a bowl, combine the chicken, smoked paprika, onion and garlic granules, parsley and some salt and pepper to taste along with a squeeze lemon juice. Cover, chill in the fridge and leave to marinate for at least 1 hour, but 15 minutes is better than nothing.
- Once the chicken has marinated, heat a frying pan over a medium heat. Spray with low calorie cooking spray and, once hot, pan-fry the chicken for 10–12 minutes on each side until browned. Remove the chicken from the pan and set to one side.
- To the same pan, over a medium heat, add the butter and garlic purée, scraping off any brown bits from the bottom of the pan.
- Pour in the cream and leave to simmer for 10 minutes.
- Add a further squeeze of lemon juice along with the Parmesan.
- Serve the chicken topped with the sauce, fresh parsley, spring onions and a few chilli flakes.

Homemade Chicken Kyiv and Wedges

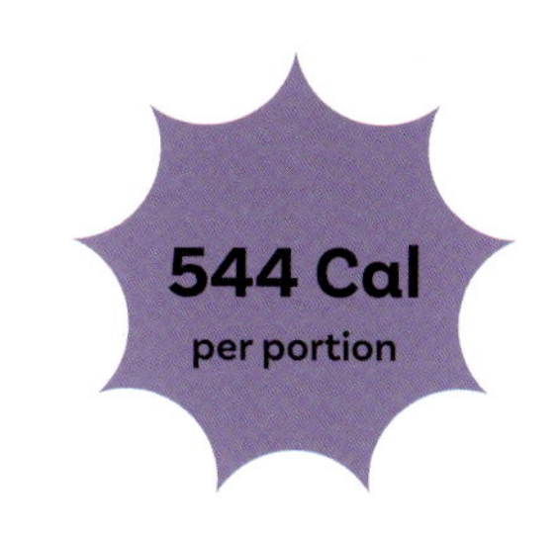

Protein 45.4g | **Fat 12.5g** | **Carbs 63.0g**

SERVES 1

TAKES 1 hour, plus 1 hour 15 minutes+ freezing

I promise homemade Kyivs may seem like a lot of work but they are really easy to make and there's no better way to elevate an already tasty dish than by drizzling barbecue sauce all over the Kyiv.

Ingredients

15g light butter, at room temperature

1 tsp garlic purée

3 sprigs of fresh parsley, chopped

120g chicken breast

1 egg, beaten

15g panko breadcrumbs

200g Maris Piper potatoes

1 tsp garlic granules

1 tsp onion granules

1 tsp dried parsley

Low calorie cooking spray

20g barbecue sauce

Salt

Salad, to serve

Method

- Mix together the softened butter, garlic and parsley. Place in clingfilm and roll tightly. Freeze for 1 hour.
- Butterfly the chicken breast and flatten, placing it on top of the clingfilm. Place the garlic butter inside, and roll the chicken tightly into a sausage shape, rolling the ends of clingfilm as you go. Place in the fridge for 1 hour or in the freezer for 15 minutes.
- Preheat the oven to 195°C/175°C fan.
- After it has chilled, unwrap the chicken and dip in the egg, followed by the breadcrumbs. Make sure that you press the breadcrumbs into the chicken firmly. Place in an ovenproof dish and set aside.
- Wash your potatoes, pat them dry, slice into wedges and season with salt, the garlic granules, onion granules and dried parsley. Spray a baking tray with low calorie cooking spray, add the potatoes and bake for 40–45 minutes until golden brown, tossing throughout.
- Bake the chicken Kyiv in the oven alongside the potatoes for 20–25 minutes until golden brown. Once the chicken is cooked, drizzle over the barbecue sauce.
- Toss the wedges in any remaining garlic butter from the Kyiv baking tray.
- Serve with a side salad.

BBQ Fajita Beef Pasta

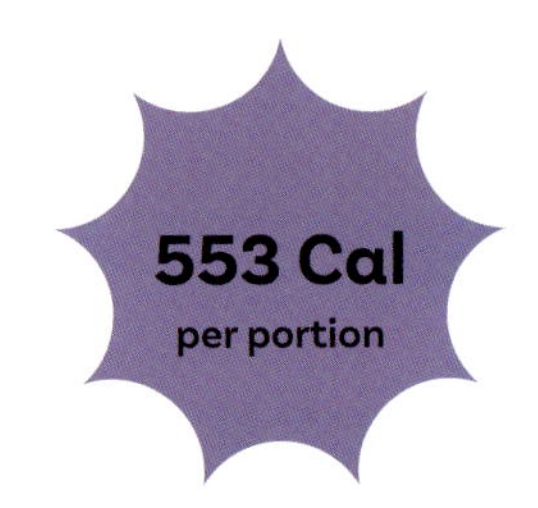

Protein 43.4g | Fat 11.5g | Carbs 66.0g

SERVES 2
TAKES 25 minutes

A quick barbecue beef fajita mince tossed in linguine, finished with a melting cheese sauce and diced chorizo for a swanky dinner.

Ingredients

15g chorizo, diced

1 red onion, diced

1 tsp garlic purée

200g lean beef mince

1 red pepper, diced

120g dried linguine

35g packet of barbecue fajita seasoning (I use Old El Paso)

45g barbecue sauce

150g passata

2 cheese singles

100ml skimmed milk

A few sprigs of fresh coriander, chopped

Salt and pepper

Method

- Start by heating a large frying pan over a medium heat. Fry the chorizo for 2–3 minutes until golden and releasing its oils, then remove from the pan.
- In the same pan, fry the onion in the garlic purée for a couple of minutes. Then add the beef mince, followed by the red pepper.
- Add the pasta to a pan of boiling salted water and cook according to the packet instructions.
- While the pasta is cooking, season the beef well with the fajita seasoning, along with salt and pepper. Add the barbecue sauce and passata and leave the mixture cooking on low.
- Make the cheese sauce in a saucepan by melting the cheese singles and milk together. Stir continuously over a medium heat for 4–5 minutes until a smooth sauce has formed. Turn up the heat if needed towards the end, to thicken further.
- Once the cheese sauce is made, drain the cooked pasta and mix together with three-quarters of the beef mixture.
- Serve the remaining beef on top of the pasta and drizzle with the cheese sauce. Top with the coriander and the cooked chorizo.

Crispy Buffalo Chicken Parm with Smashed Parmesan Potatoes and Garlic Ranch Yoghurt

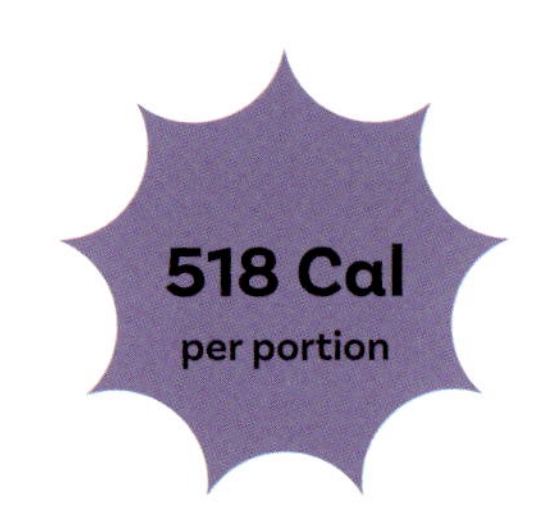

Protein 45.3g | **Fat 14.8g** | **Carbs 49.2g**

SERVES 2
TAKES 1 hour+

Dining at home does not get much better than this. While this dish does take a little longer, I promise it's super worth it for the crispy smashed potatoes and the cheesy crispy chicken. If buffalo sauce isn't your thing, sub for barbecue sauce, then serve with a rocket salad for the ultimate vibe.

Ingredients

400g baby potatoes
Olive oil spray
2 tsp garlic granules
2 x 100g chicken breasts
1 tsp smoked paprika
1 tsp onion granules
1 medium egg, beaten
30g cornflakes, crushed
15g light butter
35g buffalo sauce
60g reduced fat mozzarella, sliced
15g Parmesan, grated
Salt and pepper

Garlic ranch yoghurt
50g fat-free Greek yoghurt
½ tsp garlic granules
½ tsp onion granules
¼ tsp dried dill
¼ tsp dried parsley
1 tsp white wine vinegar

Method

- Cook the potatoes in a large pan of boiling salted water for 20 minutes. Drain in a colander and leave to rest for 5 minutes.
- Preheat the oven to 180°C/160°C fan.
- Transfer the potatoes to a large baking tray and, using the bottom of a cup, gently press down on top of the potatoes. Spray with a few squirts of olive oil, then season generously with salt, pepper and 1 teaspoon of the garlic granules. Bake in the oven for 20 minutes.
- While the potatoes are cooking, grab the chicken breasts and butterfly down the middle. Using a meat hammer, flatten the chicken breasts until they are thin.
- Season with the remaining teaspoon of garlic granules, the smoked paprika, onion granules and some salt and pepper. Rub into each breast thoroughly.
- Dip each chicken breast into the beaten egg, shake off any excess, then dip the chicken into the crushed cornflakes. Press the cornflakes into the chicken thoroughly

before shaking off and repeating on the other side. Place onto a baking tray.

- Pull the potatoes out of the oven and, using a spatula, flip over and spray again with a few pumps of olive oil.
- Put the potatoes and the chicken into the oven for 20 minutes.
- Mix together all the ingredients for the garlic ranch yoghurt and set to one side.
- When there is 10 minutes of cooking time remaining, in a saucepan melt the butter and buffalo sauce. Spoon over the chicken when there is 5 minutes of cooking time remaining, then top with the mozzarella. Scatter the Parmesan over the potatoes and return to the oven for the final 5 minutes.
- Serve the chicken on a plate with the potatoes and drizzle over the garlic ranch yoghurt sauce.
- **Air fryer** – Follow the instructions in step 3, then cook the seasoned boiled potatoes in the air fryer basket at 180°C for 15 minutes. While the potatoes are in the air fryer, follow steps 4, 5 and 6, which should take around 10 minutes. Flip the potatoes, before transferring the coated chicken into the air fryer basket with the potatoes, trying to ensure there is space surrounding the chicken. Cook for 18 minutes. Follow steps 9–11.

Mexican Cheesy Bean Jacket Potato

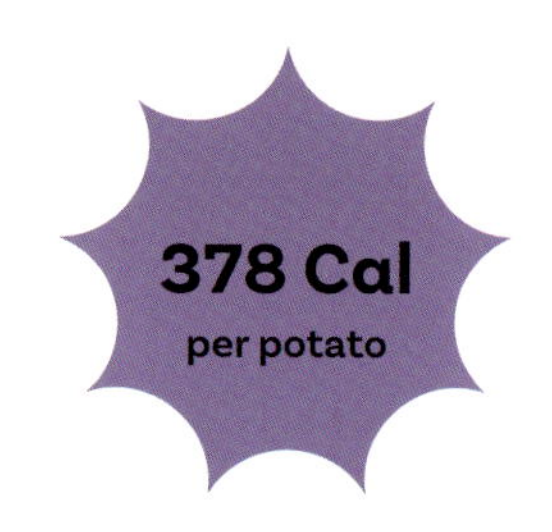

Protein 15.5g | **Fat 4.7g** | **Carbs 65.0g**

SERVES 2
TAKES 1 hour+

The humble jacket potato and beans just got a major upgrade. Refried beans and a taco chipotle cheese sauce pair beautifully with the crispy skin and fluffy inner potato. Top with some lean beef mince to boost the protein!

Ingredients

2 large golden potatoes (around 250–300g each)

Low calorie cooking spray

200g refried beans

1 tbsp tomato salsa

2 tsp taco seasoning

2 cheese singles

2 tbsp skimmed milk

½ tsp chipotle paste

A few sliced jalapeños from a jar

2 sprigs of fresh coriander, chopped

Method

- Preheat the oven to 180°C/160°C fan.
- Scrub the potatoes clean and pat dry with kitchen paper, then place them on a baking tray. Spray lightly with low calorie cooking spray and bake in the oven for 50 minutes. Turn partway through.
- Remove the potatoes from the oven and carefully cut lengthways, leaving enough skin around the edges. Scoop out 1 tablespoon of potato to leave a boat shape and set to one side.
- Add the refried beans, salsa and 1 teaspoon of the taco seasoning to a saucepan over a medium heat. Mix together and cook for 4 minutes.
- Once the beans are cooked, add half into the potato skins, top with the scoops of potato flesh that were removed earlier and add the remaining beans on top.
- Add the cheese singles, milk, chipotle paste and remaining teaspoon of taco seasoning to a microwavable bowl. Blast in the microwave for 15 seconds, remove and whisk together. Add to the top of the potatoes, drizzling down the centres quickly before it starts to solidify.
- Garnish with the jalapeños and coriander to serve.

Chicken and Chorizo Risotto

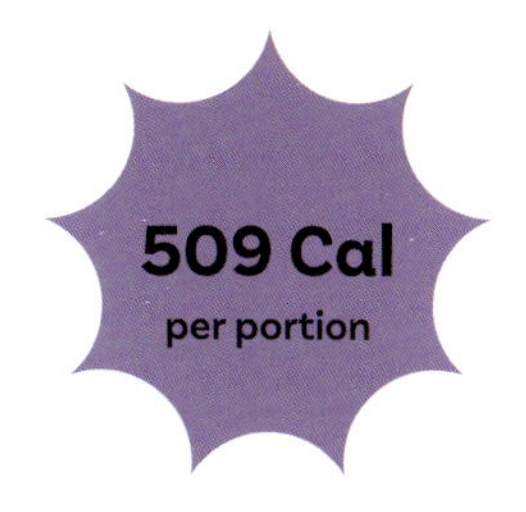

Protein 46.8g | **Fat 12.1g** | **Carbs 54.8g**

SERVES 2
TAKES 40 minutes

I love one-pan recipes. They are easy to make and there are also fewer dishes involved and to wash up. It's a win-win scenario. Chicken and chorizo is one of my favourite combinations for a risotto; top it with melted Cheddar cheese and you've got yourself a winning chicken dinner.

Ingredients

200g chicken breast, diced
2 tsp smoked paprika
2 tsp garlic granules
2 tsp onion granules
2 tsp dried oregano
20g chorizo, diced
1 red onion, diced
2 tbsp tomato purée
120g risotto rice
2 chicken stock cubes, crumbled
500ml water
50g reduced fat Cheddar, grated
10g Parmesan, grated
3 sprigs of fresh parsley, finely chopped
Salt and pepper

Method

- Season the chicken in 1 teaspoon each of smoked paprika, garlic granules, onion granules and oregano, and add salt and pepper to taste. Rub in thoroughly and leave to one side.
- In a large frying pan, over a medium heat, fry the chorizo for 3–4 minutes. Remove from the pan and set aside.
- In the same pan, cook the onion over a medium heat for 3 minutes until slightly soft. Add the chicken and fry until the chicken has cooked through.
- Add the tomato purée and risotto rice to the pan. Cook for a minute, then add the crumbled stock cubes, water and the remaining smoked paprika, garlic granules, onion granules and oregano. Season to taste with salt and pepper. Leave to simmer over a medium heat for 20 minutes or until the rice has cooked through. Add more water if needed.
- When the risotto is ready, top with the grated cheeses and cooked chorizo. Still on the heat, cover the top of the pan for a few minutes until the cheeses have melted.
- Finish with a scattering of fresh parsley.

Five

CHEEKY FAKEAWAYS

Garlic Bread Meatball Marinara Sandwich

Protein 42.0g | Fat 12.0g | Carbs 62.0g

SERVES 2
TAKES 30 minutes

There's only one way to make a cheesy tomato meatball sub better and that is by turning that sub into garlic bread. If you want a cheekier bite, try a dunk of garlic herb dip.

Ingredients

200g lean beef mince
½ tsp Italian herb seasoning
½ tsp garlic granules
½ tsp onion granules
Olive oil spray
10g light butter
1 tsp garlic purée
1 tsp dried parsley
2 sub rolls
30g mozzarella, grated
2 sprigs of fresh parsley, finely chopped

Marinara sauce

Low calorie cooking spray
1 tsp garlic purée
1 small white onion, diced
150g good-quality passata
1 tsp Italian herb seasoning
1 tsp granulated sweetener
Salt and pepper

Method

- Preheat the oven to 175°C/155°C fan.
- Season the beef mince with the Italian seasoning, garlic granules and onion granules. Roll into equal balls and add to a baking tray. Lightly spray each one with olive oil. Bake for 15 minutes. Turn them over partway through cooking, tossing in the juices.
- For the sauce, coat a saucepan with a couple of sprays of low calorie cooking spray, then add the garlic purée and onion. Cook over a medium heat for 3–4 minutes until the onion has softened. Add the passata, herb seasoning, sweetener and some salt and pepper and leave to simmer over a medium heat.
- While the sauce cooks, mix together the butter, garlic purée and dried parsley in a heatproof bowl. Blast in the microwave for 15 seconds until melted.
- Cut the sub rolls in half lengthways and brush over the garlic butter. Place on a baking tray and cook in the oven for 2 minutes.
- Top the sub rolls with half the sauce, then the meatballs, the remaining sauce on top and then the cheese. Return the subs to the oven for a minute until the cheese has melted.
- Finish with the fresh parsley.

Double Mexican Chicken Smash Burgers

Protein 38.2g | Fat 14.0g | Carbs 35.0g

SERVES 2
TAKES 25 minutes

When I say every single bite of this burger is incredible, I mean it. Each burger has two homemade double patties that are smashed with cheese and topped with pico de gallo and a homemade zesty chipotle sauce. You can make these patties ahead of time and freeze if you want to save time.

Ingredients

250g 5% fat chicken mince

4 sprigs of fresh coriander, chopped

¼ red onion, diced

1 tsp taco seasoning

1 tsp lime juice

2 brioche buns

2 slices of reduced fat Cheddar

1 little gem lettuce, finely chopped

Salt and pepper

Chipotle yoghurt sauce

40g fat-free natural yoghurt

¼ tsp lime juice

½ tsp chipotle paste

Pinch of salt

½ tsp garlic granules

Pico de gallo

¼ red onion, diced

2 sprigs of fresh coriander, chopped

1 salad tomato, diced

Pinch of salt

1 tsp lime juice

Method

- First, make the yoghurt sauce and pico de gallo by mixing all the ingredients together in 2 separate bowls. Set to one side.
- To the chicken mince, add the chopped coriander, red onion, taco seasoning and lime juice, along with a pinch of salt and pepper.
- Roll into 4 equal balls (see Note), then transfer to a frying pan set over a medium heat. Squash down into patties, using baking paper to cover and a spatula to press down. Cook for 4 minutes on each side.
- While the burgers cook, lightly toast the brioche buns.
- Add a cheese slice to 2 of the patties, leave for a minute and then top with the remaining patties.
- Add some of the chipotle yoghurt sauce to the bottom of each brioche bun, then add lettuce, the stacked chicken patties and top with the pico de gallo. Drizzle with the remaining sauce.

The burger mixture will be wet. You can either flour your hands or dampen them with water to make rolling the burgers easier.

Animal-style Loaded Chips

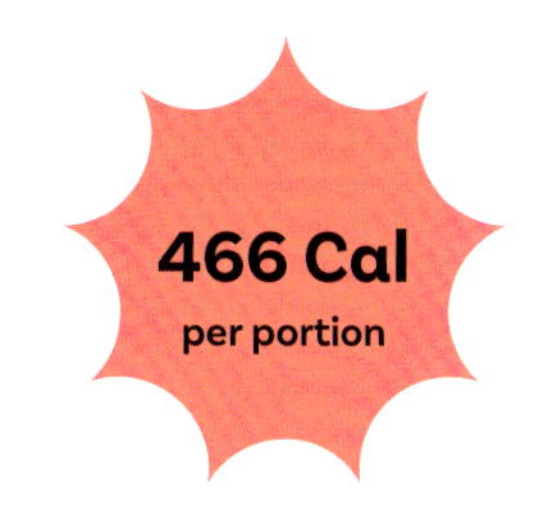

Protein 36.7g | Fat 11.3g | Carbs 53.4g

SERVES 2
TAKES 1 hour+

In this recipe fries are topped with slices of cheese and caramelised onions, then smothered in sauce. Traditionally these don't have beef mince but I like to add it as a protein source. Otherwise you could make them as a side dish to your beef burgers.

Ingredients

400g potatoes
1¼ tsp garlic granules
1¼ tsp onion granules
Low calorie cooking spray
1 large onion, diced
1 pickle, diced
80g lighter than light mayonnaise
25g reduced sugar tomato ketchup
1 tbsp white wine vinegar
1 tbsp pickle juice
1 tsp French mustard
200g lean beef mince
2 light cheese singles
Salt and pepper

Method

- Preheat the oven to 200°C/180°C fan.
- Start by peeling the potatoes and cutting them into thin chip shapes. Pat dry, season with salt, pepper and 1 teaspoon each of the garlic and onion granules. Spray them thoroughly with low calorie cooking spray. Place the chips in a single layer on a baking tray and bake in the oven for 45–50 minutes until fully cooked, turning over twice during cooking.
- While the chips cook, add half the onion to a frying pan over a medium heat. Continuously keep adding water after a couple of minutes until the onions are golden brown. Set aside.
- Add the remaining onion to a bowl with the diced pickle, mayonnaise, ketchup, white wine vinegar, pickle juice and a pinch of salt. Mix well, add the mustard and loosen slightly with water to get a thinner sauce.
- When the chips are almost cooked, spray a clean frying pan with cooking spray and fry the mince over a medium heat, seasoning in the pan with salt, pepper and the remaining garlic and onion granules.
- Preheat the grill to low.
- Once cooked, top half the chips with the mince, then the remaining chips and the cheese. Melt under the grill, then finish with the sauce and cooked onions.
- **Air fryer** – Cook the chips at 190°C for 25 minutes.

Hot Honey Chicken and Pepperoni Pizza

Protein 50.9g | Fat 15.0g | Carbs 53.5g

MAKES 1 pizza/**SERVES** 2
TAKES 40 minutes

Once you know how easy homemade pizzas are to make, your life will change. I told you hot honey is delicious and it's even more delicious with pepperoni baked on a pizza.

Ingredients

200g chicken breast
1 tsp smoked paprika
1 tsp garlic granules
1 tsp onion granules
½ tsp dried oregano
100g self-raising flour
120g fat-free Greek yoghurt
40g tomato and herb pizza sauce
30g pepperoni slies
1 red pepper, sliced
1 red onion, sliced
50g ready-grated mozzarella and Cheddar mix
25g runny honey
1 tsp hot sauce
1 tsp water
1 tsp dried parsley
Chilli flakes (optional)

Method

- Preheat the oven to 180°C/160°C fan.
- Season the chicken thoroughly with the smoked paprika, garlic granules, onion granules and oregano and pop in the oven on a lined baking sheet for 17 minutes. Once cooked, cut into small pieces.
- While the chicken cooks, combine the flour and yoghurt until you have a soft dough. Roll out to your desired thickness (roll out thinner if you are sharing) and place on an oiled baking tray. Pop in the oven alongside the chicken for 5 minutes.
- Once the base is part-cooked, remove from the oven and top with the pizza sauce, chicken chunks, pepperoni, pepper, onion and cheese. Bake for a further 15–20 minutes.
- Mix together the honey, hot sauce and add the water to loosen. Once cooked, drizzle the sauce over the pizza and sprinkle with the parsley and some chilli flakes if you like it HOT.

Please use thick authentic Greek yoghurt and not the runny style, otherwise the dough will be too wet to roll.

Cajun Philly Cheesesteak Wraps

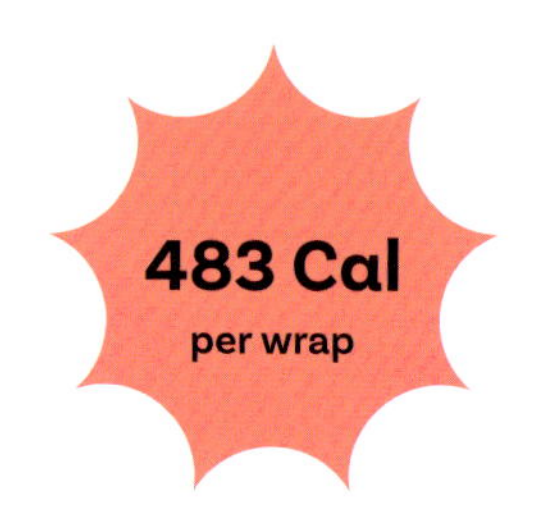

Protein 38.8g | Fat 18.0g | Carbs 37.0g

MAKES 2
TAKES 20 minutes

Cheesy, full of thinly sliced Cajun beef, and all tucked up into a crispy golden wrap, each bite is perfection. If you like more heat, jalapeños also work really well in these wraps but that isn't for the faint hearted. Pair with smashed potatoes, fries or a huge side salad, depending on your goals.

Ingredients

200g rump steak, fat removed
1½ tsp Cajun seasoning
Low calorie cooking spray
1 tsp garlic purée
1 small white onion, sliced
1 small green pepper, sliced
½ tsp smoked paprika
30g mozzarella, grated
2 tortilla wraps
30g reduced fat Cheddar, grated
Salt and pepper

Method

- Cover the beef with clingfilm and, using a meat mallet or rolling pin, gently pound the meat from the centre outward to create a thinner steak.
- Season the beef with 1 teaspoon of the Cajun seasoning and some salt and pepper. Rub it in thoroughly on both sides.
- Spray a frying pan with low calorie cooking spray, add the beef and cook over a high heat for 1 minute on each side. Remove from the pan and leave to rest.
- Turn down the heat to medium, add the garlic purée, onion and green pepper and fry for a couple of minutes until soft.
- Using a sharp knife, thinly slice the beef on the diagonal.
- Once the veggies are soft, add the smoked paprika, the remaining ½ teaspoon of Cajun seasoning and some salt and pepper and mix well. Return the beef to the pan, top with the mozzarella and cook until it has melted.
- Lightly warm the wraps in the microwave for 10 seconds.
- Divide the Cheddar equally between the wraps, top with the steak and fold the wraps. Pan-fry for 2–3 minutes on each side until golden.

Peri Peri Chicken Flatbread

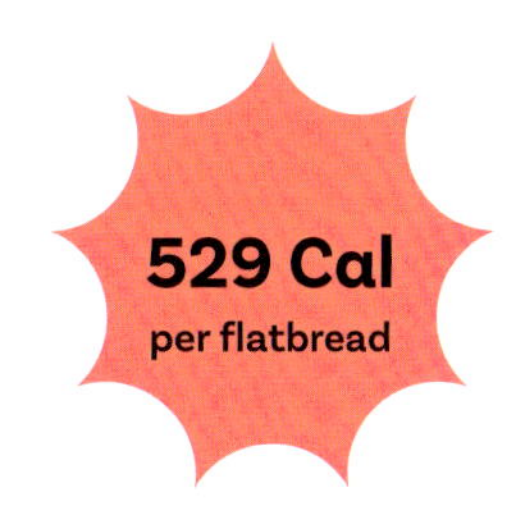

Protein 37.8g | **Fat 13.8g** | **Carbs 62.1g**

SERVES 2

TAKES 25–30 minutes

Juicy peri peri chicken, soft red onion, peppers and crispy fries all tucked into soft fluffy flatbreads drizzled in peri peri mayonnaise. Fully loaded, these flatbreads require both hands to eat.

Ingredients

200g chicken breast

1 tsp smoked paprika

1 tsp garlic granules

1 tsp dried oregano

1 tsp lemon juice

1 tbsp plus 1 tsp peri peri sauce

1 red pepper, thinly sliced

1 red onion, thinly sliced

100g frozen fries

2 flatbreads

100g lettuce, shredded

40g peri peri mayonnaise (I use Nando's Perinaise)

A few sprigs of fresh parsley, chopped

Salt and pepper

Method

- Preheat the oven to 180°C/160°C fan.
- Season the chicken with the smoked paprika, garlic granules, oregano and some salt and pepper, rubbing in thoroughly. Place on a lined baking tray and brush over the lemon juice and the 1 tablespoon of peri peri sauce. Bake in the oven for 20 minutes. When there is 5 minutes of cooking time remaining, add the pepper and onion to the baking tray.
- Meanwhile, cook the fries according to the packet instructions.
- Once the chicken is cooked, thinly slice it into strips.
- Build the flatbreads with the shredded lettuce, red pepper and onion, fries and sliced chicken. Drizzle the ½ teaspoon of peri peri sauce over each flatbread and follow with the peri peri mayonnaise and parsley.
- **Air fryer** – Cook the seasoned chicken at 180°C for 17 minutes.

Butter Chicken Garlic Naan

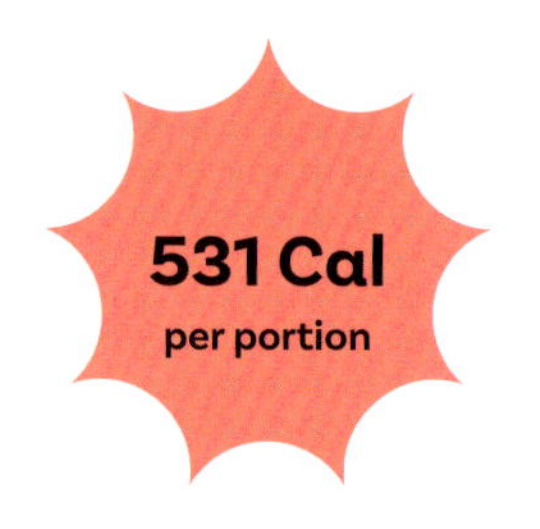

Protein 45.3g

Fat 12.6g

Carbs 58.4g

SERVES 2

TAKES 40 minutes

A homemade soft garlic and coriander naan loaded full of butter chicken curry; ditch those takeaway menus because this recipe has got those cravings covered. Don't be put off by the list of ingredients for this recipe; it is really straightforward and the result is so worth it.

Ingredients

20g light butter

1 white onion, diced

½ tsp ginger purée

1½ tsp garlic purée

½ tsp garam masala

¼ tsp ground cumin

¼ tsp smoked paprika

¼ tsp ground turmeric

100ml chicken stock

150g tinned chopped tomatoes

Low calorie cooking spray

120g self-raising flour

130g fat-free thick Greek yoghurt

1 tsp garlic granules

1 tsp dried coriander

50ml reduced fat single cream

1 tsp granulated sweetener

4 sprigs of fresh coriander, chopped

Salt

Butter chicken

200g chicken breast, diced

¼ tsp ginger purée

¼ tsp garlic purée

40g fat-free Greek yoghurt

¼ tsp garam masala

¼ tsp ground cumin

¼ tsp mild chilli powder

¼ tsp ground turmeric

1 tbsp lemon juice

Method

- In a bowl, mix together the butter chicken ingredients: the chicken, ginger purée, garlic purée, yoghurt, garam masala, cumin, chilli powder, turmeric and lemon juice. Marinate for at least 1 hour.
- Put a frying pan over a medium heat, add 10g of the butter and cook until melted. Add the onion and fry for 3 minutes until slightly softened, then add the ginger purée, ½ teaspoon of the garlic purée, the garam masala, cumin, smoked paprika, turmeric and a pinch of salt. Fry for a further couple of minutes until the spices release their fragrance. Add the chicken stock and chopped tomatoes, then turn down to a medium-low heat.
- Spray a separate pan with low calorie cooking spray, add the marinated chicken pieces and cook over a medium heat for 10 minutes, turning occasionally.
- While the chicken is cooking, add the flour, yoghurt, garlic granules and dried coriander to a mixing bowl. Mix, using your hands, until mostly combined and forming a dough ball. Split the ball in half, then press each piece down to make a circular shape. Roll out using a rolling pin to resemble the shape of a naan.

- Remove the sauce from the heat and blitz in a blender for 30 seconds to create a smooth sauce. Return to the pan and set over a low heat, then add the cream, sweetener and the cooked chicken.
- Wipe clean the frying pan that the chicken was cooked in. Spray with low calorie cooking spray and add the first naan. Pan-fry for a couple of minutes on each side. Remove from the pan and repeat with the remaining naan.
- Once the naans have cooked, in a microwavable bowl melt together the remaining 10g of butter and teaspoon of garlic purée for 10 seconds. Stir through half of the fresh coriander and brush equally over each naan.
- Load the butter chicken on top of the naans and finish with the remaining coriander.

Lamb Kofta Kebabs

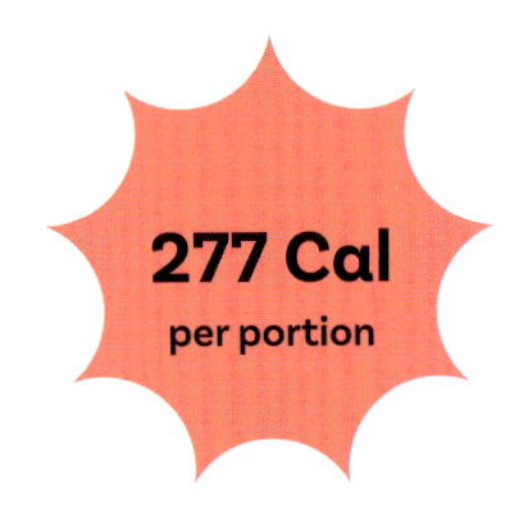

Protein 28.3g | **Fat 13.0g** | **Carbs 12.3g**

SERVES 2
TAKES 20 minutes

Juicy (tick), bursting full of flavour (tick), these lamb koftas will transport you to summer. You can swap out the lamb for beef mince for a lighter option. Pair them with a Lebanese flatbread piled high with salad or reserve them for a barbie!

Ingredients

200g 10% less fat lamb mince

½ white onion, grated

1 tsp panko breadcrumbs

1 tsp garlic purée

1 tsp chopped fresh coriander

1 tsp ground cumin

1 tsp ground coriander

1 tsp smoked paprika

¼ tsp ground cinnamon

½ tsp dried mint

Low calorie cooking spray

Salt and pepper

Yoghurt sauce

70g fat-free Greek yoghurt

1 tsp garlic granules

¼ tsp salt

1 tsp lemon juice

½ tsp dried parsley

Method

- Mix together all the ingredients for the yoghurt sauce and set to one side.
- Put the lamb mince in a mixing bowl. Add the grated onion, breadcrumbs, garlic purée and chopped coriander. Mix together well, then add the cumin, ground coriander, smoked paprika, cinnamon and mint and season with salt and pepper.
- Using damp hands, roll into a ball, then split into 4 equal balls. Roll into sausage-like shapes.
- Spray a large frying pan with low calorie cooking spray and set over a medium heat.
- If you are using metal skewers, thread a kofta onto each skewer. If you are using wooden skewers, please soak them in water for 30 minutes prior to use to prevent burning. Place the skewers in the frying pan. Cook for 4 minutes over a medium-high heat, then carefully turn the meat over using an oven glove. Cook for a further 4 minutes until browned all over and there is no visible pink meat left.
- Drizzle over the yoghurt sauce for the tastiest bite!

Loaded Gyros Bowl

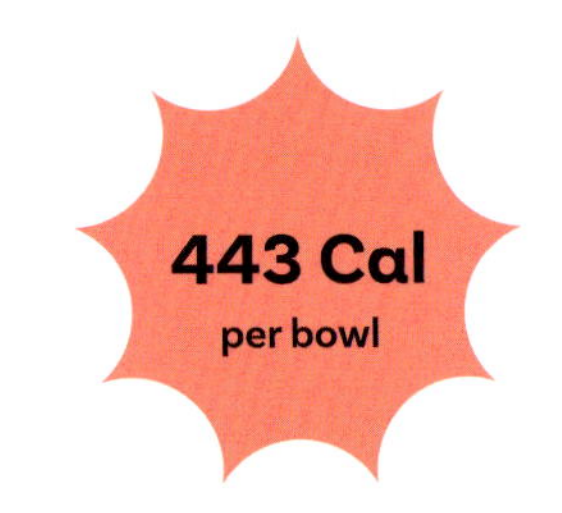

Protein 58.0g | Fat 13.4g | Carbs 22.1g

SERVES 2
TAKES 30 minutes

This recipe takes all of the flavours from the traditional gyros wrap and loads it all into a tasty healthy bowl. Packed with chicken, crispy pitta chips, golden halloumi and hummus, along with your favourite salad, these bowls are full of tasty bites.

Ingredients

300g chicken breast, thinly sliced

1½ tsp smoked paprika

1 tsp dried oregano

½ tsp ground cumin

½ tsp ground coriander

1 tsp garlic purée

1 tbsp lemon juice

2 tbsp fat-free Greek yoghurt

1 pitta bread

Low calorie cooking spray

1 tsp smoked paprika

1 tsp dried oregano

80g reduced fat halloumi , sliced

30g reduced fat hummus (or swap for tzatziki)

Salad of your choice

Salt and pepper

Method

- Add the sliced chicken breast to a bowl. Season with the smoked paprika, oregano, cumin, coriander and some salt and pepper, then add the garlic purée, lemon juice and yoghurt. Combine well, cover and leave to marinate in the fridge. For best results, leave for 4–6 hours or overnight.
- When you are ready to cook the chicken, preheat the oven to 200°C/180°C fan. Then, using 2 skewers, thread the chicken onto both ends until completely filled. If using wooden skewers, soak the skewers in water for 30 minutes to prevent them from burning in the oven.
- Place the skewers on top of a grill rack placed on a baking tray. Carefully place in the oven and bake for 15 minutes, then turn over and bake for a final 5 minutes. If there are juices beneath the chicken, brush the chicken with the juices. Leave to rest for a few minutes before thinly slicing.
- For the pitta chips, grab your pitta bread and, using scissors, cut down the middle. Cut around the edges to cut the pitta bread in half and then into triangles.
- Place the triangles on a baking tray and spray both sides with low calorie cooking spray. Season with the smoked paprika, oregano and a pinch of salt, then bake in the oven for 5 minutes until crispy.
- Next, spray a frying pan with low calorie cooking spray. Add the halloumi to the pan and fry over a medium heat for 3–4 minutes until golden on both sides.
- Serve the chicken in a bowl with the pitta chips, halloumi, hummus and your favourite salad on the side.
- **Air fryer** – Cook the marinated chicken at 200°C for 20 minutes. Spray with low calorie cooking spray a few times throughout to keep the chicken juicy.

Chilli Beef Enchiladas

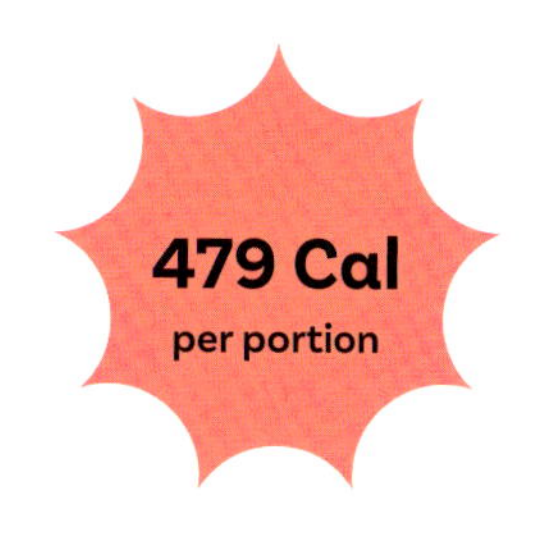

Protein 42.2g | Fat 13.9g | Carbs 45.3g

SERVES 2
TAKES 45 minutes

Crispy rolled tortillas packed full of comforting chilli with a cheesy top, these enchiladas are absolutely banging. You could easily make up a batch of chilli ahead of time and assemble when you are ready to eat.

Ingredients

Low calorie cooking spray
200g lean beef mince
1 small white onion, diced
1 tsp garlic purée
1 tsp smoked paprika
1½ tsp ground cumin
1 tsp ground coriander
1 tsp dried oregano
1 tsp mild chilli powder
150g passata
1 beef stock cube, crumbled
100ml water
4 mini tortilla wraps
40g tomato salsa
40g reduced fat Cheddar, grated
15g Greek yoghurt
2 fresh coriander sprigs, finely chopped
4 jalapeños from a jar
Salt and pepper

Method

- Spray a frying pan with low calorie cooking spray. Add the beef mince, onion and garlic purée and fry over a medium heat for 10 minutes until the beef is almost browned.
- Add the smoked paprika, cumin, coriander, oregano and chilli powder and season with salt and pepper. Mix well for a minute, then add the passata, stock cube and water. Cook over a medium heat for 5–10 minutes.
- Add the tortilla wraps to a separate pan and fry for a minute on each side until slightly toasted.
- Preheat the oven to 180°C/160°C fan and spray a baking dish with low calorie cooking spray.
- On a board, divide the beef chilli equally between the wraps. Fold over, then place into the baking dish, seam-side facing up.
- Divide the salsa equally between the wraps, followed by the grated cheese. Bake in the oven for 15 minutes until the cheese has melted.
- Drizzle over the Greek yoghurt and scatter over the chopped coriander and jalapeños to serve.

Salt and Pepper Chicken Wrap

Protein 37.7g | Fat 8.3g | Carbs 68.2g

SERVES 2
TAKES 25 minutes

This recipe is perfect for when you're craving a takeaway. Salt and pepper chicken and chips, plus curry sauce, all rolled into a flatbread. I am sure you will rinse and repeat this beauty on weekends.

Ingredients

200g chicken breast

1½ tsp Chinese five spice

15g cornflour

130g frozen chips

Low calorie cooking spray

1 white onion, cut into chunky pieces

1 red chilli, diced

1 green chilli, diced

1 green pepper, thinly sliced

1 tsp garlic purée

25g Chinese curry concentrate paste (I use Goldfish brand) mixed with 75ml water

2 flatbreads

Salt and pepper

Method

- In a bowl, season the chicken with 1 teaspoon of the five spice and ½ teaspoon each of salt and pepper. Add the cornflour, mixing in with your hands.
- Cook the chips according to the packet instructions.
- Spray the chicken lightly with low calorie cooking spray and pan-fry over a medium heat for 4–5 minutes until golden on each side. Remove from the pan.
- In the same frying pan over a medium heat, add the onion, red and green chilli, green pepper and garlic purée and fry for a few minutes until the onion has softened.
- Add the curry sauce mixture to a saucepan and stir over a low heat.
- Once cooked, add the chicken and chips to the frying pan with the onion, pepper and chilli. Mix with the remaining five spice and some salt and pepper for around 2 minutes.
- While this cooks, lightly toast the flatbreads.
- Add the chicken and chips to the flatbreads. Pour over the curry sauce and voilà!
- **Air fryer** – Cook the coated chicken at 185°C for 13 minutes, shaking the basket regularly throughout.

Sweet Potato and Chickpea Curry

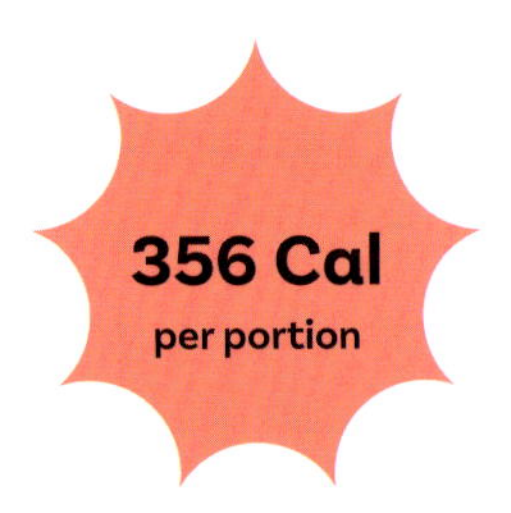

Protein 10.0g | Fat 5.1g | Carbs 55.4g

SERVES 2
TAKES 30 minutes

This is a mouthwatering veggie curry that I like to serve over rice or roti to scoop up the curry. For my non-veggie readers, chicken can be added for a protein boost if needed.

Ingredients

Low calorie cooking spray

1 white onion, diced

1 tsp garlic purée

1 tsp ginger purée

1½ tbsp mild curry powder

100g tinned chickpeas, drained

160g frozen sweet potato chunks, slightly thawed

1 tbsp tomato purée

300g tinned chopped tomatoes

100ml light coconut milk

Handful of spinach

Salt and pepper

Method

- Spray a frying pan with low calorie cooking spray. Over a medium heat, sauté the onion for 3–4 minutes until slightly softened.
- Once the onion has softened, add the garlic purée, ginger purée, curry powder and some salt and pepper to taste and mix well for a further minute.
- Add the chickpeas, sweet potato, tomato purée, chopped tomatoes and coconut milk. Mix well and leave to simmer for 15–20 minutes until the sweet potato is tender. If the sauce thickens too much, add a splash of water to loosen.
- Stir through the spinach until slightly wilted, then serve!

Crunchy, Tortilla-coated Chicken Wrap

Protein 41.4g **Fat 15.0g** **Carbs 46.0g**

SERVES 2

TAKES 30 minutes

If you haven't tried chicken coated with tortilla chips, you are in for a treat. They make such a delicious crunchy coating for chicken. Slice the chicken before pairing with a homemade creamy spicy sauce, cheese and shredded lettuce for a wrap that dreams are made of.

Ingredients

200g chicken breast

2 tsp smoked paprika

2 tsp onion granules

2 tsp mild chilli powder

30g chilli-flavoured tortilla chips (I use Chilli Heatwave Doritos)

1 egg

Low calorie cooking spray

2 wraps

50g lettuce, shredded

40g reduced fat Cheddar, grated

Salt and pepper

Sauce

60g lighter than light mayonnaise

20g reduced sugar tomato ketchup

10g sriracha

½ tbsp white wine vinegar

Pinch of salt

1 tbsp water

Method

- Preheat the oven to 190°C/170°C fan and line a baking tray with baking paper.
- Season the chicken with 1 teaspoon each of the smoked paprika, onion granules and chilli powder, and some salt and pepper. Rub in thoroughly.
- Crush the tortilla chips in a bag and season with the remaining smoked paprika, onion granules and chilli powder and some more salt and pepper.
- Pour the tortilla chips into a bowl, and in a separate bowl, beat the egg. Dip the chicken into the egg and then the crushed crisps. Push in thoroughly to make sure that the crisps adhere to the chicken. Spray each coated breast lightly with low calorie cooking spray and transfer to the lined baking tray. Bake in the oven for 20 minutes, turning halfway through.
- While the chicken cooks, mix all the sauce ingredients together in a bowl and set to one side.
- Once the chicken is cooked, cut it into strips.
- Slice the wraps partway down the middle and add the lettuce, sauce, chicken and cheese to each quarter. Fold each quarter on top of each other. Heat a frying pan over a medium heat and pan-fry the wraps for a couple of minutes on each side until golden.
- **Air fryer** – Cook the seasoned chicken at 185°C for 17 minutes.

Smoky Black Bean Burgers with Hot Sauce Mayo

Protein 17.5g | Fat 12.5g | Carbs 49.5g

MAKES 2
TAKES 30 minutes

Perfect for meat-free Mondays, these bean burgers have got you covered. Mixed with Tex Mex flavours and finished with a mouthwatering sauce, each bite is truly delicious.

Ingredients

130g tinned black beans

1 tsp ground cumin

¼ tsp smoked paprika

3 sliced jalapeños from a jar, roughly chopped

30g sweetcorn, roughly chopped

1 spring onion, diced

1 tsp light soy sauce

¼ tsp garlic paste

1 tsp lime juice

½ egg, beaten

20g dried breadcrumbs

Olive oil spray

2 cheese singles

2 brioche buns

100g lettuce, shredded

½ red onion, sliced

Salt and pepper

Sauce

40g lighter than light mayonnaise

3 tsp hot sauce

1 tsp jalapeño juice from the jar

⅛ tsp smoked paprika

⅛ tsp garlic granules

Method

- Preheat the oven to 180°C/160°C fan and line a baking tray with baking paper.
- Drain the black beans and pat dry. Using a fork or a potato masher, mash the beans. Be careful not to overmash – you still want some texture to the beans.
- Season the black beans with the cumin, smoked paprika and some salt and pepper. Fold in the chopped jalapeños, sweetcorn and spring onion, then add the soy sauce, garlic paste and lime juice.
- Once the mixture is combined, add the beaten egg, followed by the breadcrumbs.
- Roll the bean mixture into 2 equal balls and transfer to the lined baking tray.
- Carefully press down and mould the edges of each ball to create a burger shape. Spray with olive oil spray and bake in the oven for 15 minutes.
- While the bean patties are cooking, mix together all the ingredients for the sauce and set to one side.
- When the patties are ready, top each one with a cheese slice and return to the oven for a few minutes. While the cheese is melting, lightly toast the brioche buns.
- Spread half of the sauce on both bottom buns, top with the shredded lettuce, a bean patty, red onion and the remaining sauce.

Million Dollar Mac and Cheese

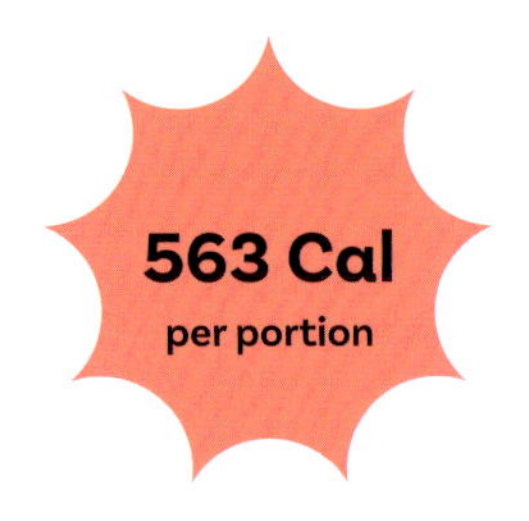

Protein 25.7g | **Fat 22.0g** | **Carbs 64.2g**

SERVES 2

TAKES 30 minutes

Why is it a million dollars you may ask? That's because this recipe is seriously addictive. It is creamy and cheesy, with an added crunch from the crackers. Using smoked cheese provides flavour that would usually come from meat, and Red Leicester cheese gives a sharp tang for an added taste sensation. If you want to add meat, top with lean diced bacon and omit the crackers.

Ingredients

- 20g light butter
- 20g plain flour
- 250ml skimmed milk, warm
- 120g dried macaroni
- 1 tsp smoked paprika
- 1½ tsp garlic granules
- 1 vegetable stock cube, crumbled
- ¼ tsp Dijon mustard
- 30g smoked cheese, grated
- 30g Red Leicester, grated
- 4 cheese crackers, crushed
- 2 sprigs of fresh parsley, chopped
- Salt and pepper

Method

- In a saucepan, melt the butter, then gradually whisk in the flour. Using a jug, slowly add the warm milk bit by bit, whisking to ensure a smooth mixture.
- Cook the macaroni in a large pan of boiling salted water according to the packet instructions.
- Preheat the oven to 180°C/160°C fan.
- Once the béchamel sauce starts to become smooth, add the smoked paprika, garlic granules, a pinch of salt and pepper, the stock cube and mustard. Continue to whisk until smooth.
- Off the heat, stir through the smoked cheese. If the sauce becomes too thick, add a tablespoon of pasta cooking water.
- Drain the pasta and combine with the sauce, then pour into a baking dish and top with the grated Red Leicester and the crackers.
- Bake in the oven for 20 minutes until the edges are bubbling.
- Serve with the fresh parsley scattered over the top.

Crispy Honey Soy Shredded Chicken

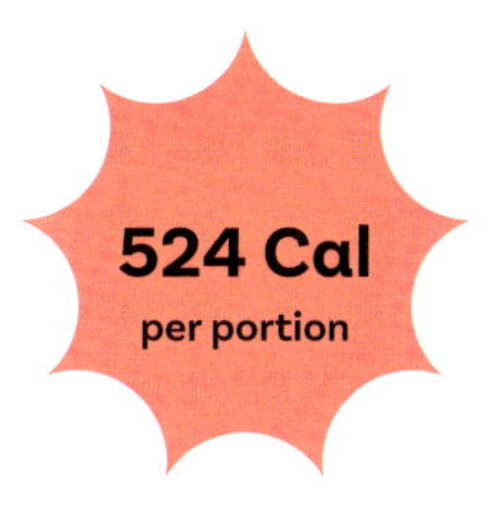

Protein 36.2g | **Fat 5.6g** | **Carbs 79.0g**

SERVES 2

TAKES 40 minutes

AF

Crispy thin strips of chicken coated in a sweet and savoury sauce, this is the total fakeaway vibe for dinner. Add some prawn crackers for a cheekier fakeaway or steamed pak choi for an added health kick.

Ingredients

200g chicken breast, cut into thin strips

2 tsp garlic purée

1 tbsp light soy sauce

½ tsp sesame oil

Pinch of black pepper

1 medium egg white

Low calorie cooking spray

25g cornflour

125g packet of boil-in-the-bag long-grain rice

1 white onion, sliced

1 red pepper, sliced

2 spring onions, chopped

1 red chilli, sliced

Stir-fry sauce

1½ tbsp light soy sauce

1 tbsp dark soy sauce

1 tbsp fresh lemon juice

30g runny honey

Pinch of chilli flakes

1 tbsp water

Method

- Add the chicken to a mixing bowl, then add 1 teaspoon of the garlic purée, the light soy sauce, sesame oil and black pepper. Mix well and leave to marinate for 15 minutes, then add the egg white and mix to combine.
- Preheat the oven to 190°C/170°C fan.
- Spray a large baking tray with low calorie cooking spray, then dip each piece of chicken into the cornflour to coat. Place the chicken on the baking tray, making sure that there is no overlap.
- Spray the chicken with low calorie cooking spray and bake in the oven for 20 minutes until crispy, making sure to spray the chicken with cooking spray and turn it partway through.
- Cook the rice according to the packet instructions.
- While the rice is cooking, mix together all the ingredients for the sauce and set to one side.
- When there is 5 minutes cooking time remaining on the chicken, spray a frying pan with low calorie cooking spray. Over a medium heat, sauté the remaining teaspoon of garlic purée, the onion, red pepper and half the spring onions for 5 minutes until softened.
- Add the sauce and cook for 2 minutes, then stir in the cooked chicken.
- Serve the chicken over the rice, garnished with the remaining spring onion and the chilli.
- **Air fryer** – Cook the coated chicken at 190°C for 12 minutes, shaking throughout.

Veggie Ramen

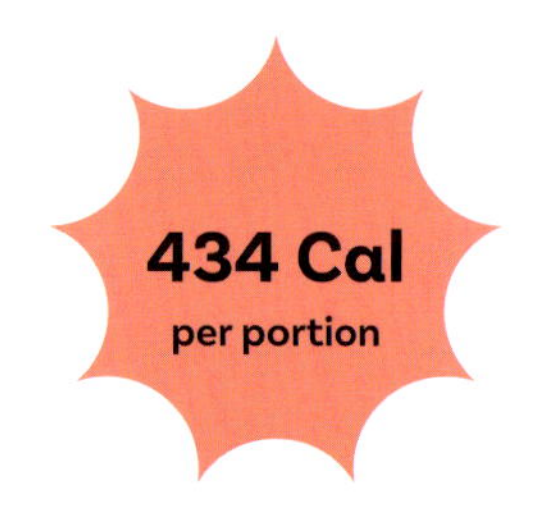

Protein 20.6g | Fat 13.0g | Carbs 59.3g

SERVES 2
TAKES under 30 minutes

When I backpacked in Japan, I couldn't get enough ramen and I knew one had to be included in this cookbook. A warm soupy broth with plenty of noodles and a deep umami flavour, this is such a comforting meal. Pork or chicken are my favourite types of meat to add if you want added protein.

Ingredients

Low calorie cooking spray
100g shiitake mushrooms, sliced
1 tsp sesame oil
1 tsp ginger purée
1 tsp garlic purée
2 tbsp light soy sauce
1 tbsp rice wine vinegar
1 tsp gochujang paste
3 spring onions, sliced
800ml vegetable stock
2 medium golden-yolk eggs
1 tsp miso paste
1 baby pak choi, quartered
2 ramen noodle nests
Chilli oil, for drizzling

Method

- Spray a frying pan with low calorie cooking spray. Add the mushrooms and fry over a medium heat for a few minutes.
- Meanwhile, add the sesame oil and ginger and garlic purées to a large saucepan and fry over a medium heat for 2 minutes.
- To the same pan, add the soy sauce, vinegar, gochujang paste and half the spring onions. Fry for a further 2 minutes, then add the stock and fried mushrooms.
- While the stock is cooking, bring a small saucepan of water to the boil. Over a high heat, boil the eggs for 7½ minutes. Remove the eggs and place them in an ice bath for 3 minutes. This will make the shells easier to peel.
- Add 2 tablespoons of the stock mixture and the miso paste to a small bowl. Mix together to make a slurry, then add back into the stock.
- Add the pak choi to the frying pan you cooked the mushrooms in, add a little water and cook for a couple of minutes. Take off the heat.
- Add the ramen noodle nests to the broth and cook for 3 minutes.
- Divide the noodles equally between 2 bowls, pouring over the broth. Add the pak choi around the edges.
- Using a spoon, gently crack the edge of each egg. Remove the shell by peeling under the membrane very carefully so as to not pierce the yolk.
- Halve the eggs and place on top of the ramen. Serve with the remaining spring onion and a drizzle of chilli oil.

Gochujang Crispy BBQ Chicken Burgers

Protein 40.8g | Fat 7.7g | Carbs 52.4g

SERVES 2
TAKES 25 minutes

A fusion of flavours come together for one of the best-tasting chicken burgers I have had the pleasure of devouring. Homemade chips are perfect with this recipe to scoop up any extra sauce.

Ingredients

2 chicken breasts
1 tsp smoked paprika
½ tsp ginger purée
½ tsp garlic purée
30g cornflakes
1 tsp garlic granules
1 egg, beaten
25g barbecue sauce
1 tsp gochujang paste
2 light cheese singles
2 brioche buns
50g lettuce, shredded
¼ tsp sesame seeds
1 spring onion, diced

Sauce

40g lighter than light mayonnaise
10g gochujang paste
1 tsp lime juice
40g fat-free Greek yoghurt
1 tbsp sriracha sauce

Method

- Preheat the oven to 180°C/160°C fan.
- Season the chicken lightly with ½ teaspoon of the smoked paprika. Brush over the ginger and garlic purées.
- Crush the cornflakes in a freezer bag, and season with the remaining smoked paprika and the garlic granules. Dip the chicken in the beaten egg followed by the cornflakes. Press in to adhere.
- Transfer the coated chicken to a baking tray and bake in the centre of the oven for 25 minutes.
- While the chicken cooks, mix together all the ingredients for the sauce in a bowl, and set to one side.
- In a separate bowl, mix together the barbecue sauce and gochujang paste. Cover and blast in the microwave for 30 seconds so that it is warm.
- Once warmed, brush the barbecue and gochujang sauce over the cooked chicken, top each breast with a cheese single and return to the oven for a further minute.
- Lightly toast the buns and fill with half the sauce, lettuce, chicken, more sauce, sesame seeds and spring onion.
- **Air fryer** – Place the coated chicken in the air fryer (straight into the drawer, or on a silicone liner) and cook at 185°C for 18 minutes.

Loaded Creamy Chicken Garlic Baguette

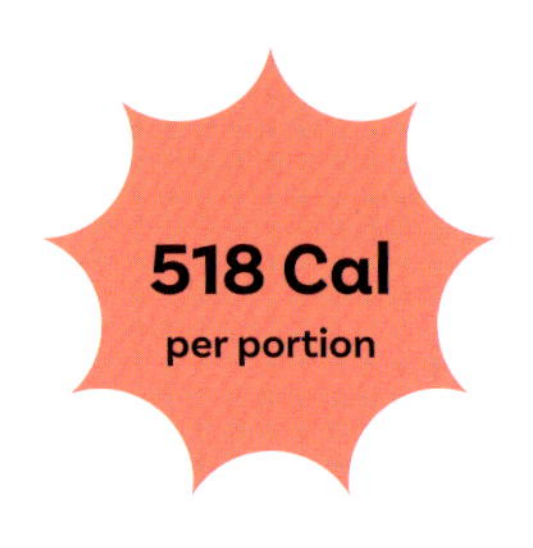

Protein 48.5g **Fat 14.2g** **Carbs 47.8g**

SERVES 2
TAKES 25 minutes

Baked garlic bread topped with seasoned chicken, smoky bacon, a homemade creamy sauce and melted mozzarella gives layers of flavour. If you fancy making it a little bit extra, drizzle over some ranch sauce.

Ingredients

Low calorie cooking spray
40g lean bacon, diced
200g chicken breast, diced
2 tsp garlic granules
2 tsp onion granules
½ tsp smoked paprika
½ tsp dried oregano
1 bake-at-home white sourdough baguette
20g light butter
10g plain flour
150ml skimmed milk, warm
1 tsp garlic purée
1 tsp dried parsley
40g mozzarella, grated
3 sprigs of fresh parsley, chopped
Salt and pepper

Method

- Preheat the oven to 180°C/160°C fan.
- Spray a frying pan with low calorie cooking spray, add the bacon and pan-fry over a medium heat for 7 minutes until cooked through. Remove from the pan and set to one side.
- Season the chicken with 1 teaspoon of the garlic granules, 1 teaspoon of the onion granules, the smoked paprika, ¼ teaspoon of the oregano and some salt and pepper. Ensure the chicken is fully coated before adding to the frying pan. Fry the chicken over a medium heat for 10 minutes until it is cooked through.
- Meanwhile, slice the baguette in half and bake for 8 minutes.
- Add 10g of the butter to a saucepan and cook until slightly melted. Add the flour and mix together with the melted butter. Once the butter and flour are combined, start to gradually whisk in the milk. Keep stirring until it thickens, then season with the remaining garlic granules, onion granules and oregano, and some salt and pepper. Mix until well combined.
- Carefully remove the baguette from the oven. Mix together the remaining 10g butter, the garlic purée and dried parsley and brush over the baguette halves, covering as much surface as you can.
- Top each baguette half with the chicken and bacon, then pour over the creamy sauce, making sure the surface is covered. Top with the mozzarella and bake for a further 4 minutes.
- Remove from the oven and garnish with the fresh parsley.

Chicken Souvlaki Wraps

Protein 42.4g | **Fat 15.0g** | **Carbs 40.0g**

SERVES 2
TAKES 25 minutes

Simple yet utterly delicious. The chicken is pan-fried over a high heat to give that BBQ effect; don't worry, it is still juicy thanks to marinating in lemon juice. These wraps are paired with an easy tomato, onion and feta filling to get those taste buds going. Swap to pork or try hummus rather than tzatziki if you want to change things up.

Ingredients

200g chicken breast, cut into chunks
1 tsp smoked paprika
1½ tsp dried oregano
1 tsp garlic purée
1 tbsp lemon juice
2 salad tomatoes, sliced
1 small white onion, sliced
30g feta, chopped
1 tbsp red wine vinegar
¼ tsp salt
Olive oil spray
2 Greek flatbreads
100g tzatziki

Method

- In a bowl, mix together the chicken, smoked paprika, 1 teaspoon of the oregano, the garlic purée and lemon juice. Leave to marinate in the fridge for 1 hour if possible. If you only have 10 minutes, that will do.
- In a bowl, mix together the tomatoes, onion, feta, vinegar, remaining oregano and the salt and combine.
- When you are ready to cook the chicken, spray a pan with olive oil and set the heat to medium-high (the oil should be sizzling slightly). Add the chicken pieces in a single layer. Cook undisturbed for a few minutes before flipping; there should be a slight char. Turn down the heat slightly and fry for 10 minutes until the chicken is completely cooked.
- Remove the chicken from the pan. Add each flatbread in turn to toast slightly.
- Take each flatbread, top with the chicken, tomato mixture and the tzatziki. Roll and wrap in baking paper or foil to hold them together.

Six

HAVE A PUDDING!

Mini Vanilla New York-style Cheesecakes

Protein 8.0g | Fat 6.0g | Carbs 9.5g

MAKES 8

TAKES 30 minutes, plus 1 hour+ chilling

These mini cheesecakes are highly addictive and do not taste like they are made healthier at all. They are baked to get the proper cheesecake bite but I promise they are simple to make and store well (if you can resist devouring them all).

Ingredients

60g digestive biscuits

15g light butter

200g light cream cheese, at room temperature

115g fat-free thick Greek yoghurt, at room temperature

2 tsp vanilla extract

25g granulated sweetener

1 medium egg, at room temperature

Method

- Preheat the oven to 160°C/140°C fan and line a muffin tray with 8 silicone moulds.
- Crush the biscuits into a fine crumb. You can do this by placing the biscuits into a sandwich bag or something similar and using a rolling pin.
- Blast the butter in the microwave for 10 seconds before adding to the biscuits. Mix well.
- Divide the biscuit mixture equally between the moulds and use the back of a teaspoon to press it down.
- In a mixing bowl, combine the cream cheese, yoghurt, vanilla extract and sweetener until smooth. Add the egg and stir until just combined. Spoon the mixture into each mould. Once filled, tap the tray to release air bubbles.
- Bake in the oven for 20 minutes.
- Remove from the oven and leave to cool slightly. Place in the fridge for at least 1 hour before devouring. Keep in the fridge for up to 4 days, or freeze for up to 3 months.

Retro School Cake

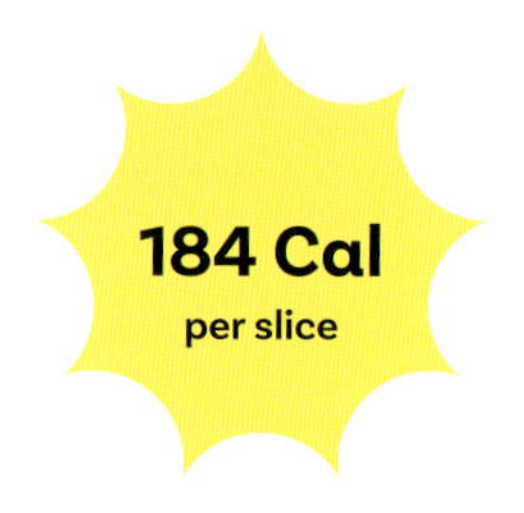

Protein 6.0g | Fat 4.5g | Carbs 34.0g

MAKES 9 thick slices

TAKES 40 minutes, plus cooling

Let's face it, this cake was the best thing about going to school. Eating lower-calorie puddings shouldn't mean we have to scrimp on taste and, let me tell you, you are going to be shocked at how easy and delicious this cake is.

Ingredients

Low calorie cooking spray (optional)

2 medium eggs, at room temperature

50g fat-free Greek yoghurt

100ml skimmed milk, warm

20g light butter, melted

1 tsp vanilla extract

180g self-raising flour

40g caster sugar

20g granulated sweetener

1 tsp baking powder

Pinch of salt

100g royal icing sugar

20g colourful sprinkles

Method

- Preheat the oven to 180°C/160°C fan and grease a 20cm square baking tin with low calorie cooking spray. Alternatively, line the tin with baking paper.
- In a bowl, whisk the eggs until smooth, then add the yoghurt, milk, melted butter and vanilla extract.
- In a separate bowl, sift the flour, then add the caster sugar, granulated sweetener, baking powder and salt. Stir to combine.
- Gently fold the dry ingredients into the wet ingredients. Add the batter to the prepared baking tin, smoothing it out using the back of a spoon until the tin is covered.
- Bake in the centre of the oven for 20–25 minutes until golden and a toothpick inserted into the centre comes out clean.
- Leave the cake to cool for 15 minutes, then remove from the tin and leave to cool for a further 10 minutes.
- Add the icing sugar to a bowl, then add a tablespoon of hot water at a time and mix until a thick icing has formed. This usually requires 2–3 tablespoons of water.
- Spread the icing over the surface of the cake so that it is completely covered. Scatter over the colourful sprinkles and leave for 5 minutes to set.
- Slice into 9 equal slices. Store in an airtight container for up to 4 days.

Cinnamon Sugar Donut Balls

Protein 3.2g | Fat 0.8g | Carbs 10.1g

MAKES 8
TAKES 30 minutes

You no longer need to go to a funfair to get your sweet donut fix. These donut balls are so easy to make and ready in less than 30 minutes. If you're feeling extra cheeky, go ahead and drizzle over some chocolate sauce and serve with ice cream.

Ingredients

110g self-raising flour

150g fat-free thick Greek yoghurt

1 small egg, beaten

15g light soft brown sugar (or caster sugar)

½ tsp sweet cinnamon

Low calorie cooking spray

Method

- Preheat the oven to 180°C/160°C fan and line a baking tray with baking paper.
- In a mixing bowl, mix together the flour and yoghurt. Once combined, use your hands to form a large ball.
- Cut the dough ball in half, then into quarters. Roll each quarter into an equal ball. Take some dough from each ball so each piece makes 2 balls – you should have 8 balls in total. They will expand in the oven. Don't worry if the dough is slightly sticky – this is the texture we need for the donuts.
- Roll the dough balls until smooth, then place onto the lined baking tray. Brush over the beaten egg
- Bake in the oven for 15 minutes, then turn over and bake for a further 5 minutes until golden.
- Mix together the brown sugar and cinnamon.
- Once the donut balls are cooked, spray each one with low calorie cooking spray, then roll in the cinnamon sugar. Dust off any excess.
- Best served immediately.
- **Air fryer** – You don't need to brush the donut balls with the beaten egg if using an air fryer. Spray the air fryer drawer with low calorie cooking spray or line with baking paper. Cook the donut balls at 180°C for 10 minutes.

Make sure you use authentic thick Greek yoghurt, not just Greek-style as this will result in a wetter mixture which will not form into balls.

Dark Chocolate Frozen Yoghurt Cups

Protein 6.5g | **Fat 5.6g** | **Carbs 8.1g**

MAKES 9
TAKES 15 minutes

Smooth, creamy frozen yoghurt with a peanut butter swirl and a crunchy chocolate topping, these cups are easy, delicious and versatile. Some of my other favourite variations are caramelised biscuit spread and caramel sauce in place of the peanut butter, adding a scoop of vanilla protein powder for an added protein boost. Add nuts for a chunky-style cup or, for those hot days, try adding some crushed fruit to the mixture.

Ingredients

300g fat-free thick Greek yoghurt
1 tsp vanilla extract
1 tbsp granulated sweetener
20g smooth peanut butter
60g dark chocolate
1 tsp coconut oil

Method

- Line a muffin tray with 6 silicone moulds.
- In a mixing bowl, mix together the yoghurt, vanilla extract and sweetener. Divide equally between the silicone moulds.
- Meanwhile, put the peanut butter in a microwavable bowl and blast in the microwave in 20-second intervals until slightly melted. Alternatively, add a couple of tablespoons of hot water to loosen. Add a small amount of peanut butter to the centre of each mould. Swirl around using a toothpick.
- Add the dark chocolate and coconut oil to a microwavable bowl and again blast in intervals until melted. Add on top of the yoghurt mixture using the back of a small spoon to spread over the top to cover.
- Place in the freezer for at least a few hours to harden. Keep the cups stored in the freezer and pull out for a couple of minutes prior to eating to soften slightly.

Chocolate Brownie 'Ice Cream'

Protein 19.0g | Fat 7.0g | Carbs 21.5g

SERVES 2

TAKES 10 minutes, plus 6 hours+ freezing

I could easily sit and inhale a tub of ice cream on a Friday night, but most are super high in calories. This healthier version made with Greek yoghurt hits that sweet spot guilt-free. I like to reuse Greek yoghurt pots to give me the full ice-cream-tub vibe but normal Tupperware works fine too. Switch the cocoa powder to hot chocolate powder for more of a milk chocolate taste, or use a scoop of chocolate protein powder for an extra protein hit.

Ingredients

300g fat-free Greek yoghurt

30g cocoa powder

60ml almond milk

2 tsp vanilla extract

1 tbsp granulated sweetener

3 mini fudge brownie bites

Method

- Add the Greek yoghurt, cocoa powder, almond milk, vanilla extract and granulated sweetener to a blender. Blitz until smooth. Alternatively, mix the ingredients together in a bowl.
- Chop the brownie bites into small pieces.
- Pour the Greek yoghurt mixture into a freezer-friendly container (see intro). Add half of the brownie pieces to the mixture, then stir and top with the remaining pieces.
- Freeze for at least 6 hours. When you are ready to eat, pull out the ice cream for 5 minutes prior to eating and use an ice-cream scoop to dish up.

Cookies and Cream Brownies

Protein 4.9g | Fat 7.6g | Carbs 16g

MAKES 12
TAKES 35 minutes

These are the best lower-calorie brownies with the richest chocolate flavour. Mixed with crushed cookies-and-cream biscuits and chopped dark chocolate, this is a pudding that will definitely satisfy any sweet cravings!

Ingredients

2 large eggs
20g granulated sweetener
20g light butter, melted
80ml skimmed milk
115g dark chocolate, chopped
100g self-raising flour, sifted
20g cocoa powder, sifted
¼ tsp salt
½ tsp baking powder
6 cookies and cream biscuits (I use Oreos), crushed

Method

- Preheat the oven to 180°C/160°C fan and line a baking tray (around 28 x 22cm works best) with baking paper.
- In a stand mixer or a bowl using an electric whisk, whisk together the eggs and sweetener for 4 minutes until fluffy. Add the melted butter along with the milk, then whisk for a further 30 seconds until combined.
- Add 100g of the dark chocolate to a microwavable bowl. Heat for short blasts in the microwave until the chocolate has melted.
- Once the chocolate has melted, add to the egg mixture and whisk until combined.
- Fold in the flour, cocoa powder, salt and baking powder, followed by half of the crushed biscuits and the remaining 15g of chocolate.
- Add the batter to the baking tray, ensuring the surface is smooth. Sprinkle over the remaining crushed biscuits.
- Bake in the centre of the oven for 16–18 minutes. Take a toothpick and insert it into the centre to check that the brownie has cooked. It should come out clean with a few crumbs surrounding it.
- Remove from the oven and leave to cool slightly before slicing into 12 equal squares. Store in an airtight container at room temperature for up to 3 days.

Apple Crumble

Protein 4.0g | **Fat 5.8g** | **Carbs 39.3g**

SERVES 1
TAKES 30 minutes

The homeliest comforting pudding there is. Delicious as it is, or serve it with a dollop of Greek yoghurt or low fat ice cream, and for those darker evenings add a little sprinkle of cinnamon over the top.

Ingredients

1 red apple (around 100g peeled weight)

1 tsp granulated sweetener

1 tsp lemon juice

⅛ tsp ground cinnamon

½ tsp cornflour

50ml water

Low calorie cooking spray

Crumble

20g rolled oats

10g plain flour

10g light butter

1 tbsp granulated sweetener

1 tbsp skimmed milk

Method

- Peel and dice the apple into small cubes. Add to a saucepan, then add the sweetener, lemon juice, cinnamon and cornflour. Mix to combine and pour in the water. Set over a medium heat for 10 minutes, with a lid to cover.
- Preheat the oven to 180°C/160°C fan.
- Meanwhile, in a bowl, mix together the oats, flour, butter, sweetener and milk. for the crumble. Using your fingertips, rub the mixture together to create a dough-like texture.
- Once the apple is slightly tender, transfer it to a small ovenproof ramekin. Top with the crumble mixture, ensuring all of the apple is covered.
- Spray with low calorie cooking spray, then bake in the oven for 20 minutes, or until the apple is completely tender.

Double Chocolate Chip Muffins

Protein 5.4g | Fat 4.8g | Carbs 16.0g

MAKES 8
TAKES 35 minutes

Fluffy, rich, super chocolatey and dare I say it 'moist', these muffins are the perfect pud! The coffee used in this recipe intensifies the chocolatey flavour, although you can't taste it, but it is totally optional if you want to leave it out.

Ingredients

Low calorie cooking spray (optional)

2 large eggs, at room temperature

20g light butter, melted

20g granulated sweetener

70g fat-free thick Greek yoghurt, at room temperature

1 tsp vanilla extract

60ml skimmed milk

1 tsp lemon juice

140g self-raising flour

15g cocoa powder

¼ tsp salt

¼ tsp bicarbonate of soda

1 tsp coffee granules (optional)

15g dark chocolate, chopped

20g milk chocolate chips

Method

- Preheat the oven to 220°C/200°C fan and line a muffin tray with 8 silicone moulds. Alternatively, spray 8 muffin holes with low calorie cooking spray, ensuring they are well greased to prevent sticking.
- In a mixing bowl, whisk together the eggs, melted butter and sweetener until combined.
- Stir through the yoghurt and vanilla extract until there are no lumps left from the yoghurt, then mix through the milk and lemon juice.
- Using a sieve, first add the flour, followed by the cocoa powder, salt, bicarbonate of soda and coffee granules, if using. Fold the dry ingredients into the wet ingredients, ensuring they are all incorporated evenly.
- Fold in the dark chocolate and half of the chocolate chips.
- Divide the mixture evenly between the silicone moulds. Top each muffin with the remaining chocolate chips.
- Place the tray in the centre of the oven for 5 minutes, then reduce the temperature to 180°C/160°C fan and bake for 18 minutes. The muffins are ready when a toothpick inserted into the centre comes out clean.
- Leave the muffins to cool for 15–20 minutes before digging in. Store in an airtight container for 3 days.

If using a muffin tray with empty holes, fill the other holes with water-filled silicone moulds to ensure even cooking.

Eton Mess

Protein 11.9g | Fat 2.1g | Carbs 22.3g

MAKES 2
TAKES 10 minutes

I knew there had to be a quick and simple pudding in this book, something to make after a long day. Using Greek yoghurt makes this pud a lot lighter. It's sweetened to complement the other ingredients with a dollop of squirty cream to add back some indulgence. So... what are you waiting for?

Ingredients

200g strawberries

2 meringue nests

200g Greek yoghurt

1 tsp vanilla extract

1 tsp granulated sweetener

20g light squirty cream

Method

- Wash the strawberries, remove the stalks and roughly chop. Add half to a blender and blitz into a purée. Alternatively, place in a bowl and use a fork to mash half of the strawberries.
- Break the meringue nests into pieces.
- In a bowl, mix together the Greek yoghurt, vanilla extract and sweetener. Fold in half of the strawberry purée and half of the chopped strawberries.
- Now it is time to layer! Dollop half of the yoghurt mixture into 2 individual glasses, top with half of the meringue pieces, the remaining yoghurt mixture and remaining meringue. Add the remaining chopped strawberries, the squirty cream and drizzle over the remaining strawberry purée.
- Serve as soon as possible!

Golden Chocolate Speculoos Truffles

Protein 1.4g | Fat 3.4g | Carbs 10.0g

MAKES 5 balls

TAKES 20 minutes, plus chilling

These truffles are so simple you'll wonder why you don't always have a batch in the fridge. Smooth, creamy and no-bake, you really can have a pud ready in no time.

Ingredients

50g speculoos biscuits (I use Biscoff)

30g lightest cream cheese (I use Philadelphia)

40g golden caramel chocolate (I use Cadbury Caramilk), broken into pieces

Method

- Blend the biscuits in a food processor. Alternatively, place in a sandwich bag and crush until a fine crumb.
- Mix the crushed biscuits together with the cream cheese.
- Form the mixture into 5 balls with your hands. Place on a baking tray lined with baking paper, and pop into the freezer for 5 minutes.
- Melt the chocolate in short bursts in the microwave, or in a heatproof bowl set on top of a saucepan of simmering water.
- Once melted, roll each ball in the melted chocolate. Return to the lined baking tray and place in the fridge until the chocolate sets.

To store, keep in the fridge in a tightly sealed container lined with kitchen paper for 2–3 days.

Lighter Lemon Loaf Cake

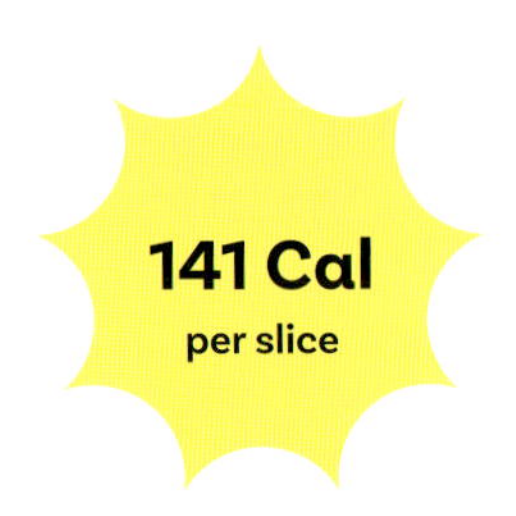

Protein 6.1g | Fat 4.3g | Carbs 25.0g

MAKES 14 slices
TAKES 40 minutes

This recipe takes me back to my nana's house where my addiction to lemon cakes began. Each bite of this bake is light, fluffy and extremely moreish. If you fancy more of a spring pudding option, blueberries and raspberries make a great addition.

Ingredients

Low calorie cooking spray
300g self-raising flour
40g granulated sweetener
1 tsp bicarbonate of soda
2 tsp baking powder
2 large eggs, at room temperature
20g light butter, melted
50g fat-free thick Greek yoghurt
100ml skimmed milk
1 tsp vanilla extract
150ml lemon juice
Zest of 1 lemon, plus extra (optional) to decorate
100g icing sugar
2 tbsp water

Method

- Preheat the oven to 180°C/160°C fan and grease a 24cm loaf tin with low calorie cooking spray.
- In a large mixing bowl, sift the flour, then add the sweetener, bicarbonate of soda and baking powder and gently combine.
- In a separate bowl, whisk the eggs, then add the melted butter, yoghurt, milk, vanilla extract and 100ml of the lemon juice. Mix until smooth.
- Gently fold the wet ingredients into the dry. Be careful not to overmix. Pour the batter into the prepared tin and top with the lemon zest.
- Bake in the centre of the oven for 20–25 minutes. The cake is ready when a toothpick inserted into the centre comes out clean.
- Leave to cool in the tin, then transfer to a wire rack.
- In a measuring jug, mix together the remaining lemon juice, the icing sugar and water until combined. Pour over the loaf cake, spreading evenly and adding more lemon zest for decoration if you wish.
- Cut into 14 equal slices to serve. Store in an airtight container for up to 4 days.

Salted Caramel Cookies

Protein 4.3g | **Fat 11.0g** | **Carbs 15.0g**

MAKES 8

TAKES 25 minutes, plus cooling

These cookies are a delicious treat that are also nutritious thanks to the ground almonds and oats. Chewy yet soft, I guarantee you will have a hard job not to polish off the whole lot!

Ingredients

55g light butter, softened

50g light or dark soft brown sugar

1 large egg, at room temperature

1½ tsp vanilla extract

85g ground almonds

½ tsp baking powder

½ tsp salt

50g rolled oats

30g white chocolate chips

20g caramel sauce

Sea salt, for sprinkling

Method

- Preheat the oven to 180°C/160°C fan and line a baking tray with baking paper.
- Ideally use either a stand mixer or a hand-held electric mixer to whisk together the butter and brown sugar on medium speed for around 30 seconds.
- Add the egg and vanilla extract and beat again on low speed for 20 seconds.
- Add the ground almonds, baking powder and salt and mix on low speed again for 20 seconds. Be careful not to overwhisk.
- Fold in the oats and the chocolate chips. Using an ice-cream scoop or your hands, roll the dough into 8 equal balls and place on the prepared tray, leaving enough room for the cookies to spread during baking.
- Bake for 12 minutes. The outsides of the cookies should be golden when you remove them from the oven and the insides still a little doughy. They will continue to cook once removed from the oven. Leave to cool for 15–20 minutes.
- Serve with the caramel sauce drizzled over and scatter each cookie with a pinch of sea salt. The cookies will keep in an airtight container for 2–3 days.

If you need to firm up the cookie dough before rolling, chill in the fridge for 10 minutes.

Index

Acknowledgements

First and foremost, thank you to Ru Merritt. Without you there would be no book! Thank you for your guidance, vision and help along the way in this journey. To Vicky Orchard, my editor, thank you for your patience and everything you have done to support me on this journey. Not forgetting Charlotte Macdonald who I began this journey with and Francesca Thompson who has helped me with the publicity and marketing for this book.

To all those who brought the book to life. Firstly, the photographer, Ellis Parrinder, food stylists, Troy Ellis and Rosie Reynolds and prop stylist Daisy Shayler-Webb. You really have captured the essence of what my food is all about and I am so incredibly grateful to have worked with you on this book. A thank you to backgrounds studio for allowing the space to create these photos.

A massive thank you to Michelle and Rosie at Studio Noel. The design of the book still blows me away when I see it. It's truly one of a kind and I feel very lucky to have had you both working on the design.

To my mum and dad, thank you for always being there no matter what, for supporting my dreams, for teaching me determination and providing me with strength. I hope I continue to make you proud with everything that I do. Alex's Kitchen Bangers was first created in my mum's kitchen and it will always be a huge part of the journey. To my fiancé, Kieren, what would I do without you? You have been my rock throughout this journey. Thank you for always making me smile, for pushing me to aim higher and believing in me every step of the way. My best friend, Robyn, without your push I would never have created my page. Thank you for your listening ear and creative advice.

Finally, a huge thank you to you, for believing in me enough to pick up this recipe book. I really wouldn't be here without you and those who follow and support my journey across social media. It really does mean the world to me to have you here. I hope this book is everything and more you need it to be.

Ebury Press, an imprint of Ebury Publishing
Penguin Random House UK
One Embassy Gardens, 8 Viaduct Gardens,
Nine Elms, London SW11 7BW

Ebury Press is part of the Penguin Random House group of companies whose addresses can be found at global.penguinrandomhouse.com

First published by Ebury Press in 2024

www.penguin.co.uk

A CIP catalogue record for this book is available from the British Library

ISBN 9781529941517

Editorial Director: Ru Merritt
Project Editor: Vicky Orchard and and Charlotte Macdonald
Design: Studio Noel
Photography: Ellis Parrinder
Food Stylists: Troy Willis and Rosie Reynolds
Prop Stylist: Daisy Shayler-Webb

Colour origination by Altaimage Ltd
Printed and bound in Italy, by LEGO SpA

The authorised representative in the EEA is Penguin Random House Ireland, Morrison Chambers, 32 Nassau Street, Dublin D02 YH68.

Penguin Random House is committed to a sustainable future for our business, our readers and our planet. This book is made from Forest Stewardship Council® certified paper